The Liberty Option

The Liberty Option

Tibor R. Machan

IMPRINT ACADEMIC

ia

Copyright © Tibor R. Machan, 2003

The moral rights of the authors have been asserted
No part of any contribution may be reproduced in any form
without permission, except for the quotation of brief passages
in criticism and discussion.

Published in the UK by Imprint Academic
PO Box 200, Exeter EX5 5YX, UK

Published in the USA by Imprint Academic
Philosophy Documentation Center
PO Box 7147, Charlottesville, VA 22906-7147, USA

ISBN 0 907845 630

Societas: Essays in political and cultural criticism
Volume 5

A CIP catalogue record for this book is available from the
British Library and US Library of Congress

Contents

Acknowledgements vi

Preface vii

Introduction
A Short Lesson About Liberty 1

Chapter 1
Why Freedom Remains The Priority 11

Chapter 2
Financing Law without Taxation 27

Chapter 3
Private Property Rights 39

Chapter 4
The Gist of a System of Liberty 63

Chapter 5
Liberty – Abstract and Concrete 67

References 95

Societas series details 98

Acknowledgements

I wish to thank several publications for permission to make use of materials in this work that appeared in works they have published by me. Among them are *The Philosophers' Magazine, Hoover Essays in Public Policy,* and *Journal des Economists et des Estudes Humaines.* I also wish to thank the Hoover Institution and its Executive Director, John Raisian, for its support of the work I have been doing on this and related projects.

Preface

This is a brief introduction to the philosophy of liberty — also dubbed classical liberalism and libertarianism in the literature of political philosophy — the political outlook that is associated with such thinkers as John Locke, Adam Smith, John Stuart Mill, Ludwig von Mises, F.A. Hayek, Milton Friedman, Ayn Rand and others. The best-known academic philosophical exponent of this view was the late Robert Nozick, of Harvard University, in his book *Anarchy, State, and Utopia*.

After a longish introduction the rest of the essays discuss certain central issues in libertarianism and the book ends with some brief — and thus mainly suggestive — thoughts about ways in which the natural rights variety of libertarianism addresses a variety of issues.

It has been pointed out to me over my career that libertarianism may be better defended on utilitarian grounds than the ones I deploy. That is to say, it is good to respect and protect individual liberty because that way the highest values of human life will be best secured and promoted.

Unfortunately, sometimes this is true but not always — at times free men and women do not secure and promote what is best for them. They may be lazy, careless, and even reckless. So, being free doesn't guarantee happiness. It is for this reason that some prominent libertarians distinguish themselves from utilitarians — the late Robert Nozick is most notable for this. The utilitarian typically will deploy force — or even become a statist — so as to secure the greatest good for all, whereas the libertarian holds that individual rights to life, liberty and property are unalienable, inviolate, even if this risks occasional setbacks on the front of promoting certain values.

Of course, if respecting the rights to life, liberty and property actually promoted human unhappiness these rights could not be defended. But that's not the issue. What is at stake is whether a principled, rights-based defense of libertarianism is sound, rather than one that requires showing, in each case where a public policy decision needs to be made, that liberty will assure the promotion of happiness. In my view the former approach is correct and so I do not think, for example, that whether or not gun control laws ought to be enacted needs to be debated every week, month or even year, based on the latest statistics as to whether places with such laws reduce or increase crime.

So, we have in these brief essays discussions of what libertarianism means and why it is, beyond a reasonable doubt, the best political system.

Introduction

A Short Lesson About Liberty

It will help me explain and defend the free society if we have a clear enough idea of what it is. As with all normative theories, the classical liberal, libertarian system has several versions, even though the tenets of the political position are not very complicated to lay out. I have gone over the following lines with several other libertarian political theorists and have not found major objections voiced against it.

Champions of the fully free society uphold the sovereignty of each adult individual in social life. They distinguish themselves in the political arena in most western countries from both the Left and the Right because, on the one hand, the Left is inclined primarily to impose restrictions on individuals pertaining to their economic or material actions, while the Right imposes on individuals when it comes to their spiritual or mental actions. Both Left and Right enlist government for the purpose of regimenting certain aspects of the individual's life, whereas the libertarian sanctions only those laws or rules that aim at keeping everyone's sovereignty — at protecting individual rights to life, liberty and property.

Just as a quick illustration, many US conservatives endorse the war on drugs as well as a closer unity between government and church, bans on prostitution, gambling, pornography and other vices. It is mostly concerning the crafting of people's souls that the Right enlists the government's coercive powers, although since body and soul aren't ever sharply divided, this often involves regulating people's economic activities as well (e.g. Sunday liquor laws).[1]

---

[1] Conservatives aren't united so much on doctrine as on ways to think about normative matters. They hold that how we decide our institutions, laws,

The Left, in turn, wants heavy government regulation of the economy — minimum wage laws, anti-trust crusades, etc.[2] They want progressive taxation and government efforts to equalize and redistribute wealth, not simply to protect the integrity of market and other voluntary transactions and interactions. Here, too, a sharp division between the economic and the spiritual is impossible, so the Left is often involved in regimenting people's talking and thinking (e.g., when it supports government bans on hate speech or racial discrimination in commerce) while the Right will often support 'blue' laws to protect people from moral degradation.

In the particular area where their philosophical focus is, the Left and Right both want government intrusion. Ayn Rand noted this a long time ago — she suggested, thereby, that metaphysics has a good deal of impact on public policy. (The Right's idealism and the Left's materialism tend to dictate what is to be controlled.)

In non-Western countries and cultures these distinctions are less germane. In the context of such societies the libertarian seems almost beyond the pale for considering individual rights the bedrock of justice, given how prevalent groupism — tribalism, ethnic or religious solidarity, nationalism and the like — tends to be.

The champion of the fully free society sees the function of the legal system and authorities as, first and foremost, to protect individual rights. In that respect the champion of the fully free society is more loyal to the (original) vision of the American republic and the English political theorist John Locke, the philosophical grandfather of that polity, than are any other political movements afoot now. Republicans, Democrats, socialists, conservatives, liberals, communitarians, Islamic, Christian, Hindu or other religious fundamentalists and the rest all seek to impose ways of private conduct, often claiming that there does not even exist a sphere of legitimate privacy in human life.

The US Declaration of Independence states, by contrast, following the lead of Locke, that all men are created equal and endowed by their creator with certain unalienable rights, amongst which are life, liberty and the pursuit of happiness. Champions of the free system believe that they flesh out this document more accurately, consistently and completely than do Democrats, Republicans, socialists, communists, communitarians or any other political faction in this society.

---

and practices should be grounded in tradition — what has worked in the past, what has been tried and found true.

[2] The Left in America, often called 'liberals', do endorse a doctrine, mainly concerning the role and scope of government in the lives of the citizenry, which is supposed to be extensive and broad, mainly so as to enable folks who aren't doing well in life to flourish.

Why? Because if we really do have the right to our lives, for example, then the legal system should protect us against all efforts on the part of either criminals, foreign aggressors or the legal authorities themselves as to how we ought to live. All paternalistic intervention, even for the sake of improving some aspect of our lives, is intolerable — bans on drug abuse and smoking in private places or regulation of employment. Adults are off limits as far as regimenting their lives, actions and goals is concerned. That is what having an unalienable right to life, liberty and the pursuit of happiness comes to, nothing less. A proper legal order has as its primary goal to protect these rights.

Take the particularly controversial case of the position that no one has the authority to prevent you from committing or seeking assisted suicide. Now that's fairly radical. Many find it objectionable because they think we either belong to God or to some group or, thus, aren't authorized to decide what happens to us and what should be done about it.

Champions of the system of liberty hold that one's right to life is the only authority to decide what happens to one's life and that if someone who can assist with suicide is invited by one to help, prohibiting it is unacceptable. The right to life, according to this view, means that you, not other people, should be the one who makes decisions about your life, including whether to delegate to someone else who is willing the authority to help with ending it.

Rights are principles identified in the field of political theory that spell out 'borders' around us. In order to cross those borders, those inside must provide those outside with permission.

Just consider the right to private property, as we normally understand it. If it is your car, somebody else who wants to use it must ask your permission. You are the one who is to make that decision. If you want to refuse permission you have the authority to do so, others do not. If you wish to sell it, that, too, is up to you and to whoever is willing to meet your price.

Similarly, if it is your life, somebody who wants to do something to it must gain your permission — as when you authorize a physician to perform a risky operation or a cabby to drive you to the airport. On the other hand if, for example, you don't want to go into the ring with a world champion boxer who wants to fight you, that, too, is properly up to you, not somebody else.

If you want to smoke, drink, take drugs, climb mountains or go skiing, provided no one else's rights are violated by such actions, you need no one's permission. That is what is so fundamental about libertarianism. Individuals are the ones who are sovereign, not the legal authorities and not even the majority of the people.

Sovereign means you rule yourself. Nobody rules you. Sovereignty is that condition under which somebody has the fundamental right to self-governance and others must ask permission before they intrude on this government. The consent of those who are to be governed is necessary before government by others than oneself can commence. That is because their lives are their own, not someone else's — the family's society's, nation's, race's, ethnic group's, gender's or humanity's. It's your decision — even if you misgovern yourself, or if you waste your life away.

People may offer you advice, write editorials directed at you, send you letters, try to talk with you — in short, they may approach you in peaceful ways. But they have no authority to take over the governance of your life.

Even democracy — meaning many, indeed, the bulk of the people — does not void this individual sovereignty. Why should it? After all, the majority is composed of individuals, and if alone they aren't authorized to intrude on your life, together they aren't either. Democracy is a method, mainly, of selecting administrators of various, including governmental, tasks. Or it is a method that can be used to reach decisions if all those affected have agreed to its use, as in the Rotary or Lions Club.

One must authorize — delegate authority to — legal administrators to do certain things. Only then do they acquire proper authority — as opposed to mere power — to do them. If the authority was not given, then the officials lack it and must stay out of your life (educational, commercial, scientific, religious, or anything else) as well as your actions — that is what having the right to liberty means.

I am free in the political sense if I can take various actions without interference by other people. (There are other senses of 'freedom' but they are not relevant here.) If I want to pursue a life of productivity, creativity, art, science or education, I may embark on those pursuits and no one may prohibit me from doing so. If others are needed by me for these pursuits, their consent is required. And if I choose not to embark upon such pursuits but, instead, choose to be idle, lazy, imprudent, neglectful toward myself and my best interests, including making contributions to my community, that is also something I have a right to do. I am not to be placed into involuntary servitude to others or to myself. Voluntary association is essential to free men and women.

One reason why so many people cower at certain points from the classical liberal position is that they think that when one's freedom is misused then some kind of governmental, forcible interference is justified. So that, for example, you want to pursue a life of laziness, drug addition or debauchery, then they think this may be forcibly prevented. But this is wrong.

The libertarian says that with the authority to run your life goes the risk that you may mismanage your life. It's up to you. Once you reach the age of reason, once you are an adult, once you are no longer in a state of dependence — upon the wisdom, insight or guidance of your parents or guardians — you are in charge of your life and community with others must be voluntary on all sides.

The legal authority within a given jurisdiction is no more than a kind of referee. It's only concerned with maintaining peace and the maximum absence of violence against individual rights, and with no one abridging those rights with impunity. That means that if someone's rights are violated, the culprit at least gets punished for the deed. Neither the legal authorities nor anyone else can always prevent the violation of rights. Just like a referee in a basketball court who cannot always prevent the players from misbehaving. But once they have misbehaved, adverse consequences follow — they must get penalized for it. So similarly, the function of the legal authority, as the classical liberal sees it, is to protect against and penalize violators of individual rights.

As adults we all have equal status — not economically, not in terms of our beauty, our background or how nice our parents are but in terms of our rights. 'All men are created equal' does not mean that we are created equally wise, smart, wealthy, lucky or beautiful. It means that we are all equally in charge of our lives.

That's why the US Declaration of Independence could be used to criticize and reform the Constitution of the United States, which tolerated slavery. In the Declaration there was no tolerance of slavery, something Thomas Jefferson realized and over the implications of which he agonized even while engaging in the practice in his private life.

The US Declaration was not a political instrument, as the Constitution was and still is and wherein a lot of compromises were and are still being made with the principles of liberty. The Declaration articulated an unblemished vision of a free society.

It is to secure our unalienable rights to life, liberty and the pursuit of happiness, among others, that government — the agency that administers the law — is established within human communities. It is not established to do anything else — to manage a post office, build monuments, run AMTRAK, conduct AIDS prevention programs, maintain parks, forests and beaches or undertake the education of children. The government of a *bona fide* free society exists to secure the basic rights that all individuals have. That is, in part, because government makes use of force and violence and those may only be used defensively, while protecting one's rights.

The question can be asked, do people really have these rights? That's *the* controversial political question. Once we have correctly identified the rights it pretty much follows that the only time that someone may use force, which is what the legal authorities — courts, police, military, bureaucracy — are professionally trained to do, is in defense of those rights. What if those rights are a fiction, a myth?

A lot of people maintain that the rights spoken of in the Declaration of Independence are contrivances. They argue that human beings do not really have such rights and that they were invented only because they serve certain special class interests. Indeed, almost all college professors construe basic individual rights to life, liberty and property as eighteenth-century myths thought up to serve certain special economic interests. Marxists, especially, think that but even those who are not Marxist have embraced this view. And they hold that in time we will see that these principles of liberty are obsolete, temporary fictions.

When you hear it said that for Cubans socialism may be a sound system, you are hearing political relativism. It says that for certain people, related to their special historical situation or particular economic or technological development, it is OK for some dictator like Fidel Castro to basically run their lives. They are not intelligent enough, or developed enough, or wise enough yet to be self-governed.

A lot of government officials at the 1996 Vienna Human Rights conference, from Africa and Asia, protested the United Nation's endorsement of the very idea of basic individual rights because, they said, that those ideas do not apply to their society. And there is widespread agreement with this idea on the part of many people in university philosophy, political science and history departments. Is there an answer to that? Well there is, at least the way that the classical liberal sees it.

There are certain things that stay stable or steady for human beings as long as there is a human race. As long as those in the fifth century BC were part of the human species — as were those in the nineteenth, are those in the twentieth or will be those in the twenty-third century — that fact of our mutual humanity will have certain ethical and political implications. So some principles of ethics and politics will be universalizable, apply throughout the human species, including that each individual is a sovereign about his or her life.

Of course, not all thinkers through all historical periods have stressed the importance of individual sovereignty. But this does not mean that individual sovereignty was not right back then or is unimportant, only that many thinkers paid little attention to it. There may be many reasons for that. For example, given that these thinkers were part of a class of people who benefitted from treating many others as if those others could be used against and not permitted to follow their own will, this is not surprising. Pointing out to the world that every individual is equally important is not always to one's vested interest.

But, given the fact of some permanent features of human nature, it is true, among other things, that no human being should be made to serve the will of another human being against his or her choice. In other words, slavery, whether it is full-scale, partial, or even minimal, has always been, and will always be, wrong when it comes to human beings. It is no excuse that in the 1900s or in Athenian Greece science, economics, sociology or politics were different, so it was OK to have slaves. No, it was wrong then and it was wrong 150 years ago and will always be so, as long as those slaves are human beings or have the characteristics of human beings — free will and moral responsibility over their lives.[3]

That is the kind of universal position that the classical liberal embraces. Not that all principles are like that, so widely universalizable. For example, how you should dress or keep clean or even rear your kids will change, based on technological, agricultural and other developments. The answers to various particular, special questions are not the same as they were 200 or 3200 years ago. These answers depend a great deal on the vehicles we drive, the kind of dwellings in which we live. Given these changes, it would be silly to maintain that there is a fundamental principle concerning those details — how we should furnish our apartments. Those matters depend too much on what are variable aspects of human life. They include a great deal of what makes up various different and equally valid human cultures.

But there are basic principles to which people elude when they say that certain values or principles of conduct do not change. The reason why the classical liberal or libertarian thinks this is right is that human beings do remain fundamentally the same throughout all those technological and related changes. No matter what the changes, our humanity remains intact.

This is the implicit idea underlying all those human rights watch groups that go from country to country, examining whether institutions like slavery or torture exist. They don't care whether it's China or Burundi or the USA or Canada. These human rights watch groups consider certain practices and policies to be inexcusable because of our fundamental humanity.

Underlying the idea of these rights to life, liberty and the pursuit of happiness — or property — is the fact of our human nature. And this nature is understood as involving as a basic fact our creativity, our need to take initiative in life, and the corresponding moral responsibility we have for living our lives properly (whatever that comes to).

For us, unlike for the rest of the animal world, there are very few instincts on which we can rely to guide us in our lives. We must dis-

---

[3] For a detailed defense of free will, see Tibor R. Machan, *Initiative — Human Agency and Society* (Stanford, CA: Hoover Institution Press, 2000) and Edward Pols, *Acts of our Being: A reflection on agency and responsibility* (Amherst: University of Massachusetts Press, 1982).

cover how to live and flourish. That's why we need education — we are not born with sufficiently detailed genetically built-in programs that guide us through life the way in which geese, cats or even the higher mammals are who do the right thing nearly automatically. We must learn that we have very few built-in measures that sustain our lives. We have to learn everything — how to eat, talk, walk, drive and the many, many far more complex tasks that amount to living human lives.

Nearly everything we do to live reasonably successful lives has to be learned by us. So we either make good use of our minds or we don't. That's the point. Human beings have the capacity to get themselves going or to fail to do so. This is fundamental to them all. Unless they are thwarted in this task by governments, criminals or invading armies, they are free either to pay heed or not to. And the right condition for their human lives is when others do not prevent this for them. Nature isn't always so accommodating but other persons can and ought to be. It is right for us all not to be intruded upon in our efforts to think through the problems that face us and to reach solutions to those problems. It is only such a community of others that is suitable to us all, when we unite on a voluntary basis.

By no means does this mean that community life is alien to us, quite the contrary. People flourish best among other people. But only if these other people do not thwart their freedom. We not only have the right to but definitely should form clubs, churches, associations, corporations and thus embark on the solutions of all of our problems and the attainment of our aspirations in the company of other persons. But only if this does not involve coercion, compulsion, the violation of these other persons' sovereignty.

Conservatives like George Will and liberals (or as they are now often called, communitarians) unite against the classical liberal or libertarian, however, on grounds that his view of human beings is too narrow. Will joins Sandel, claiming that 'much damage is done when we define human beings not as social beings — not in terms of morally serious roles (citizen, marriage partner, parent, etc.) — but only with reference to the watery idea of a single, morally empty capacity of "choice". Politics becomes empty; citizenship, too.'[4]

But this is a bogus criticism, repeated since Hegel and Marx by all those who would forcibly twist the lives of people to a vision to which they have not given their consent. Of course, human beings are 'social beings.' But this does not mean what Marx meant by it, namely, that 'The human essence is the true collectivity of man.' Rather it means that human beings live and flourish most in the company of others. But this

---

[4] George Will, 'What Courts Are Teaching', *Newsweek*, December 7, 1998, p. 98.

is something they must do by choice when they reach maturity. For the social options available to them are numerous, some suitable, some not. And they are responsible for making the right choice about what kind of social unions they will partake in.

F.A. Hayek made this point as follows:

> That freedom is the matrix required for the growth of moral values — indeed not merely one value among many but the source of all values — is almost self-evident. It is only where the individual has choice, and its inherent responsibility, that he has occasion to affirm existing values, to contribute to their further growth, and to earn moral merit.[5]

And Hayek also argues that

> The growth of what we call civilization is due to this principle of a person's responsibility for his own actions and their consequences, and the freedom to pursue his own ends without having to obey the leader of the band to which he belongs.[6]

Yes, human beings are properly held responsible for assuming various social roles in life — in their marriages, families, polities, etc. — but this responsible is empty if not chosen by them but imposed by the likes of Will and Sandel. What Will so cavalierly and callously regards a 'morally empty capacity of "choice" ', is, in fact, the absolutely indispensable prerequisite of the moral life.

In all these matters we may or may not win the prize of success. There is no guarantee. That is one of the reasons that a classical liberal or libertarian proposes a non-utopian form of community. Such an arrangement does not promise to solve all of our problems. It rests on the recognition that free men and women might not solve their problems or might do so inadequately, incompletely. They may just decide to sit there and fiddle their thumbs and watch Jerry Springer all day long. There is plenty of evidence and common sense to support this view. There is no guarantee that people will do the right thing if they are free.

Yet, it is more likely that they will discover what the right thing to do is if they are free. More so than if they are regimented around by others who have their own lives to attend to and, in any case, ought to mind their own business.

When government tells us what the minimum wage ought to be, how to run our business, what requirements we should meet to become doc-

---

[5] F.A. Hayek, 'The Moral Element in Free Enterprise,' in Mark W. Hendrickson, ed., *The Morality of Capitalism* (Irvington-on-Hudson, NY: The Foundation for Economic Education, 1992), originally written for *The Freeman*, 1962.

[6] F.A. Hayek, 'Socialism and Science', in Chiaki Nishiyama and Kurt R. Leube, eds., *The Essence of Hayek* (Stanford, CA: Hoover Institution Press, 1984), p. 118.

tors, psychologist or chiropractors, government is addressing an area that we should address in our voluntary cooperative groups.

According to the classical liberal or libertarian, that's a default position for all public policy — to wit, whatever problems or disputes arise, such as cloning, drug abuse, mental health, contagious diseases or the like, need to be dealt with peacefully, without coercive means. This will promote *bona fide* self-government in human affairs.

There are numerous issues not covered by libertarianism and left for other fields than politics to address. But there is at least one point implied by libertarianism for all areas of social life: Coercion is not suited for any of it.

You have to fill in a lot of details in order to learn the implications of the fundamental principles of physics for dealing with a particular area of the physical world. Similarly, in politics the basic principles do not tell us everything. They provide a basic framework within which we are required to solve our problems. That means that if we are going to solve problems in society, the only thing that is utterly forbidden is for me to violate your right life, liberty and property.

Within that broad framework I can consult with you, we can get together and find all sorts of solutions from biology, chemistry, zoology and physics in order to solve our problems. We may never, however, use coercion, the violation of basic individual rights.

Only within a framework of voluntary association may human problems be addressed by us, according to classical liberal or libertarian political philosophy. Once you adhere to that, there is, of course, still a whole lot of work to be done so as to flourish in life. Because simply being free of the intrusions of others is not enough to live right — it is just a precondition. You have to do useful, productive, creative, imaginative and other proper things with your freedom.

The classical liberal or libertarian, as such, does not have an answer as to how to solve all human problems. We have all the special disciplines and professions for that. The classical liberal or libertarian has answers to our political question: How should we treat each other in a community? With full, uncompromising respect for one another's rights. No violation of those rights is permitted. That prominent and widely championed objective of economic equality — actually equality with respect to most matters of value to people — is not one that suffices to trump the right to individual liberty, including the liberty to obtain and keep valuable stuff. For one, such equality is not attainable — those imposing it as it must be imposed, by force, will never be equal to those on whom it is imposed. But even when attainable, it is worthless if obtained via the violation of individual rights.

This should provide some idea as to what libertarianism amounts to and why it makes sense to many people.

Chapter 1

Why Freedom Remains The Priority

Freedom at Issue

Human liberty — in the sense that each adult person is a sovereign citizen and no one has control of others' actions without their permission — is still, objectively speaking, the highest political value, despite the relentless and often sophisticated and subtle contentions to the contrary. It is the first principle of public policy for a just human community.

With the demise of Soviet socialism, many who have favored some version of collectivist human community organization are on the warpath against what they call liberalism but must be qualified as 'classical' liberalism. This system, with which the United States of American has always been associated, is once again taking it on the chin from innumerable theorists. For various reasons that aren't logically compelling, communitarians, market socialists and some tenacious democratic socialists reject the idea that human beings live most justly and are best off when they enjoy full protection of their right to sovereignty and liberty of action. The skeptics are wrong. A natural rights-based classical liberal or libertarian polity remains the best form of human community organization ever thought of by the human mind. Why?

Before addressing this question, let me propose that if there has been a persistent failure identified throughout human social life by successive generations — either explicitly or by implication — it has been that some persons took it upon themselves to rule others. Slavery is clearly that kind of failure. Serfdom and the attendant class system is a close kin. Critics of industrialism in its early days were finding fault with what they saw as a system that was an extension of previous limitations on freedom. In so far as early industrialists relied on forcibly obtained feudal wealth and privilege, these critics had a point.[1]

No doubt, the exact characterization of the limitation by some people of the liberty of others is a point of dispute dividing those with widely differing philosophies. Just what human freedom involves and what its protection requires is one of the most widely argued points in political thought. Should we try, by means of law, to secure every person's sovereignty, regardless of how capable he or she is of exercising it? Or should we strive, by our political institutions, to alleviate all kinds of human misery and thus 'make people free' of all impediments to their flourishing in life?

The answer usually depends on several factors but mainly on the view of human nature that underlies the analysis of freedom. Suppose that persons are, so to speak, self-starters — that is have the capacity for initiating their conduct and are essentially able to spur themselves into action (which would encourage all to take the initiative as they attempt to face the challenges of their lives). In that case it is the freedom from other person's intrusiveness within their social lives that serves as the major block to their flourishing. Once protected in their right to freedom, their own efforts (and some measure of good luck) must make the difference and is expected to, since being free they could address other problems much better than if subjugated by others. If, however, we are all held back by outside forces, whether imposed by other people or by nature — so that without warding off these forces we shall remain literally helpless — then a different idea of human liberty is needed to guide our legal system so as to help us flourish.

Indeed, within the tradition of liberal political theory the central debate has concerned the very nature of the sort of liberty that ought to be of political concern to us.[2] The classical liberal wing of this tradition

---

[1] As consistent a classical liberal or libertarian as Father James Sadowsky argues for this in 'Private Property and Collective Ownership', in T.R. Machan, ed., *The Libertarian Alternative* (Chicago: Nelson-Hall, 1974), pp. 119-133. He attributes the phenomenon to the inadequate rectification of feudal injustices in emerging quasi-capitalist systems. For more on this, see Tibor R. Machan, *The Right to Private Property* (Stanford, CA: Hoover Institution Press, 2002).

[2] The former conception of freedom is usually designated as 'negative', and the latter as 'positive', suggesting that in the former case the (right to) freedom is from others' intrusiveness in one's life, actions and property, while in the latter the (right to) freedom is to do or be something. See, Tibor R. Machan, 'Moral Myths and Basic Positive Rights', *Tulane Studies in Philosophy* (1985), pp. 35-41, as well as the accompanying essays in that issue. See, also, the classic discussion by Isaiah Berlin, *Four Essays on Liberty* (London: Oxford University Press, 1969), Chapter 3.

has argued, more or less consistently, that the only type of human liberty worthy of specifically political concern[3] is negative. The modern liberal wing has not embraced this view and has, indeed, deemed it too parochial. Human 'positive' liberty means the freedom to advance toward the ideal that is fitting for oneself, usually with 'society's' help.[4] Thus the poor are not free even if no one actively oppresses them, no one steals from them to make them poor; the same holds for all those not equally positioned in life to attain their proper goals. They are free only if their impediments are promptly removed, even if this requires forcing others to serve in this mission.[5]

In this controversy classical liberals have held on to the restricted sense of the term 'human liberty', while modern liberals have held that it is best employed when used to mean much more than not being intruded upon by others. Modern liberals take it that human liberty means the condition of being enabled to make progress in one's life. Indeed, the concept of liberty or freedom for them means choosing without any serious obstacles, not just without having others restrict one's actions.

Or, the freedom modern liberals have in mind means that whatever obstacles stand in the way of a person's progress ought to be removed by whatever means are available in society. This, of course, requires that the resources to remove those impediments have to be obtained by the state and handed to those who suffer the impediments involved. Thus whereas for the old liberals the state is supposed to protect us from those who would intrude themselves upon us, for the new liberals the state must itself intrude upon us if others can make use of what they like to call our surplus wealth. From protector of our rights the state, thus, became their violator.

The difference between the two liberal positions — and there can be others but those are not germane here — pertains mostly to how each

---

[3] That is pertaining to the principles that ought to govern human actions vis-à-vis other persons in a community aiming for suitability to human flourishing.

[4] It is notable that some conservative political thinkers, e.g., Thomas Hill Green, have also subscribed to the 'positive' conception of liberty or freedom. Indeed, we can trace this conception all the way back to Plato. Consider Edmund Burke who proposed that, 'We are afraid to put men to live and trade each on his own private stock of reason, because we suspect that this stock in each man is small, and that the individuals would do better to avail themselves of the general bank of nations and of ages.' *Reflections on the Revolution in France* (Indianapolis: Hackett Publishing Co., 1987), p. 76.

[5] Even in popular discussions there is the position that someone who may not be prohibited to or prevented by others from, say, travel, but cannot afford or is otherwise unable to do it is not free to travel.

views human nature. To see what kind of liberty is indeed vital — or which conception of liberty is most appropriate — the inquiry must begin with human nature. We need to have a clear notion of what a human being is — just for being human — to learn what kind of social life is suited for human flourishing.

Skepticism about Human Nature

Yet, there is a problem here, as well. In an age when the most trendy idea in philosophy seems to be the kind of pragmatism in which talk of human nature is moot if not entirely confused, one cannot simply set off on a journey to discover human nature. First one must decide if that road is even open for travel.

Deconstructionists, cultural relativists, pragmatists and the like tell us that the road is closed, we must rely on (usually culture-bound) historical agreement, which itself is founded on little more than accident. In that case there cannot be an any answers to our inquiry about how we might best live with each other — it's all indeterminate, awaiting the outcome of helter-skelter convention.

There is indeed a political concomitant to such a view of what human nature is, namely, communitarianism. This view seems best to accommodate the rejection of the very possibility of objectivity concerning our efforts to come to know reality. Assume for a moment, as the prominent pragmatist Richard Rorty argues, that objectivity is a myth (because it would require for us to 'climb out of our minds'. Suppose that in its place we must embrace solidarity or the inter-subjective agreement we reach within our community.[6]

Then it is impossible, in principle, to stand in opposition to the group or collective with some better idea an individual may have formulated, based on his or her objective assessment of some situation. Nor is it possible to assess the respective merits of the innumerable communities that solicit our loyalty as individuals who might become their members. This is because under this view good ideas are precisely those that the group collectively proclaims to be such.[7] Since objectivity is impossible, no individual human being's mind could grasp what is true or right and set the results against the prevailing group or decide among groups. The result of the impossibility of objectivity would, in part, be political paralysis.

---

[6] Richard Rorty, *Objectivity, Relativism, and Truth* (Cambridge University Press, 1991).

[7] Practically, of course, this means that some members of the group get to make such proclamations for the rest.

Consequences of Anti-Objectivism

So the pragmatist/communitarian approach is more of an evasion than a viable answer for us. To start with, it is self-defeating because by its own tenets its own pronouncements have no general validity. It also rests on a misconception of the human mind — as if it were a tool by which we shape rather than grasp reality. We do not know by altering the world; we know by apprehending or grasping it, leaving what we grasp unchanged unless we are careless and permit our prejudices to obstruct our understanding.

Some may be able to afford an uncritical view that takes the group's judgment for granted. Most people throughout history have had the need to get glimpses of what might be best in contrast to what the group proclaimed. And the preference for the collective's opinions as against any possible individual's objectively-grounded opposition is no more than the preference of some people as against those of others, with no valid claim to better standing.

Thus it is self-annihilating to insist on the view that the community is right, since no right and wrong can be established. We must look to another source for satisfactory answers, one that makes sense of the fact that sometimes communities are right as against some of their members, and at other times they are wrong and the few opponents or even just one such rebel may be correct, based on his or her willingness and skill at being objective or, in the context of ethics or politics, just.

Communities cannot be the court of last resort — they too often judge with bias and intolerance. The idea of substituting solidarity for objectivity would render the very idea of a dissident incoherent — all that would be left is what the Soviet officials claimed, namely, mentally ill members of the collective who had to be cured so as to rejoin the group.

Human Nature Revisited

What, then, can we say about human nature that stands the test of objectivity — of meeting the standards of being true to our unprejudiced observations and experiences?

All acts of human inquiry, of the search for answers, however fruitless they may often seem, suggest an answer to our questions. Human beings are by nature creative, not merely responsive. They do things on their own initiative — that would explain better than anything else all our developments, cultural changes, diversity of approaches to life, varied philosophies and religions, as well as much of our disagreements, conflicts, even animosities. No other animal appears to change and develop its environment and life circumstances so drastically and often and be so often at odds with members of its own species concerning what is the best thing to do. We, in contrast, are always coming up with new ideas, plans and solutions to problems, even if these be little more than the rejection of proposed solutions, the abandonment of theories, the denial of answers.

Still, as the ancient Greek Cratylus, Plato's first teacher, discovered (despite his adherence to Heraclitus's relativist doctrine), one couldn't function in this world without a system of communication. Common indicators, if not outright words, need to be employed — in his case, hand signals — just to make sense to one another. So, our relentless innovations — as well as our many disagreements — demonstrate our creative nature as human individuals, while our need for and reasonably successful practice of communication testify to our occupancy of common ground, our membership of an objectively determinate species in an objectively determinate reality.

We seem to be aware of this fact of human reality in many spheres, from strictly personal relations to international economics, from law to morality, in art as well as in science. Language clearly illustrates it — we need some stable principles for understanding and clear expression, but we also need the malleability that's part of every living language. In short, there is both the diversity that comes from individuality as well as some measure of uniformity that furthers community. This would appear to attest to both a common human nature and to the essential element of the individuality of each human being. (It is just what distinguishes human beings as rational animals that also alerts us to their individuality, since to be rational requires individual effort or initiative, something that places the particular individual in a decisive role in his or her life. This also explains best the frustration about never being able to guarantee that we will get people to think along certain lines, that we will finally persuade them — they always have the free will to reject, even very good arguments, or to come up with better ones.)

Politics

What, if any, political consequences follow from this basic fact of the world?

First, we can be reasonably certain that there are some laws or principles of human community life that can serve as ideals for every human community to aspire to. By virtue of the fact that we are human beings, there would be some features every decent, just human society would have to have in common. Indeed, the concern with human rights, expressed by various international organizations, is very probably a social articulation, albeit often muddled in its details, of the realization of this fact.

Our capacity for grasping such basic principles is highly disputed by all sorts of skeptics, yet such a stance is fraught with paradoxes since it, too, aims at grasping what is what about the human situation. We may proceed, then, with the inquiry, provided we do not expect something impossible from it, namely, *the final word* on the topic of basic principles. Human knowledge is not some concluding snapshot in need of no further touch ups. It is, rather, the best assessment of the world we can come up with for our time and place. We know when what we have is the result of having done our very best. And we know enough about ourselves by now to have learned some vital facts that should guide our political communities.

Second, while we have human nature as the source of stable facts for purposes of guiding our political organization, at the very same time we accommodate, also, the fact that change must always be anticipated. That is because the basic, natural human rights we can identify based on what we know about human nature spell out borders within which we are free to live and grow in each other's company. Human rights — as expressed, for example, by the basic provisions of the American Bill of Rights — are prohibitions laid out against others, including (especially) against governments, aiming to safeguard our liberty to make changes, to keep developing on all fronts of human existence.

Liberty and Generosity

But, one might ask, if these rights are all a matter of protecting people so they may act freely, creatively, on their own initiative, what happens to those who are ill equipped, hampered — by handicaps, poverty, illness, bad fortune — in their abilities to be creative, to develop with some measure of success? Do they not have human rights to be helped? Are they not entitled to support? In the terms of some political theorists, don't those who need support have (positive) rights to welfare, security, enablement?

To see why the idea of positive rights is a confused one, we need to consider at this point the important concept of compossibility: A compossible set of rights is a set of rights that are not in conflict; they can be respected and protected for everyone. One person's positive right to health care would be protectable but only if someone else fails to be protected — goods and services are always scarce. Moreover, positive rights *necessarily contradict* negative rights. To protect the right to health care would involve not protecting the right to liberty of those who may not want to provide such health care. The negative rights position holds that while it may well be a good thing for everyone to have health care, it would be wrong to force doctors to provide it on terms to which they object, without their consent. Even if one might argue that in some drastic, emergency cases this does not hold, as a system of law upholding the set of negative rights — to life, liberty and property — is far more conducive to justice than the idea of protecting positive rights.

At most, then, what positive rights or entitlements are can only be understood, coherently, to be values sought by many, values they may obtain through their own effort or by means of other people's generosity, not as a right. Treating these values as rights or entitlements actually implies the need to place others into involuntary servitude.

Of course, the idea of a free society does not foreclose any efforts human beings want, indeed often ought, to make on behalf of others, quite the contrary. It is only free human beings who ultimately are enabled to creatively help their fellows, not because those fellows have a lean on their lives but because they are fellow human beings whose plight is understandable by those who enjoy their own capacities reasonably unimpaired.

Prospects for Flourishing

On the broad canvas of human history, persons who have been free have, in the main, been more helpful to the rest than those who have been coerced by governments to render service. Excepting perhaps some emergencies, governments ruin the plight of the needy by thwarting the creativity of the able and willing — including the creative and ambitious traits of the temporarily helpless — at least in the long run. Slaves do not make very efficient Good Samaritans, nor do they exhibit much ambition.

So the prospects for both the fortunate and the less fortunate are greater if the human right to liberty is promoted, protected, and maintained within the various legal orders that guide different human communities.

The revolution that changed the bulk of the Western world from feudal to a constitutional individualist order — attempting to secure the sovereignty not of collectives or elites but of every individual — has reached Eastern Europe, much of Asia, Latin America and even portions of Africa. This so called bourgeois revolution — when referred to be historicists such as Marxists — is the main central, crucial turnover of political institutions in recorded history, as it shifts power from groups to individual human beings. It is the revolution that rejects the essence of nearly all old orders, namely, the view that humanity is either some whole entity (deriving in part from its characterization as a Platonic ideal standing above all particular persons) or a collection of smaller groups arranged in a hierarchical order. What is put in place of these collectivist conceptions by the 'bourgeois' revolutions of the last three centuries is humanistic individualism, the view that any individual adult human being is equal in worth to any other when it comes to the possession of the rights to life, liberty and property.

Of course, to flesh out the detailed meaning of such a revolution takes time and patience and has encountered and will continue to encounter massive setbacks. The twentieth century has seen major backlashes already, in the form of fascism and communism, as well as less significant but often equally noisy attempts at small-time collectivist states (e.g., Iran's theocracy).

Nevertheless, the revolution has made an enormous impact on the world and by any reasonable assessment — which excludes, for example, measuring human flourishing by impossible, ineffable standards — has accounted for the production of a better life on earth throughout the globe. (Of course, because of population growth, this can only mean that the percentage of human flourishing has improved, even though large numbers of persons are still in dire straits).

There is no guaranteed progress in human life. Persons are capable of leading destructive as well as flourishing lives and it is always up to them, to some extend, which they will choose to lead (even if in free societies there is greater likelihood that they will make the better choices). No revolution, in any sphere, is irreversible. To sustain it must always be a feat of human effort, an effort presuming a diverse division of labor.

One such area of sustaining labor is political thought. And on that front few can doubt that in our time massive work is being done to undo the revolution. We have few prominent intellectuals, outside of the field of economics, defending the principles of the bourgeois revolution. And the economists' efforts cannot be sufficient since they lack the crucial ethical component — one can agree that laissez-faire is more productive than its economic alternatives while still disputing the moral climate that laissez-faire supposedly promotes — e.g., consumerism, hedonism, etc. One needs to show that prosperity, which laissez-faire enhances, is something worthwhile, not merely a greed-driven, crass materialism. In political philosophy there is much support for some kind of democratic socialism or, at least, the democratic welfare state. Communitarianism — that euphemistic version of socialism — is on the rise, promising a benign version of the collectivist menace. Such support usually follows conclusions about the corrosive nature of capitalism, individualism and competition. To counter such contentions it is not sufficient to reiterate that laissez-faire is economically superior to socialism, communitarianism, fascism, etc.

Communitarian Counter-Revolution

Individualism, as well, is being belittled more actively than it has been in recent decades — usually by distorting it to mean some kind of legacy of atomism. Books by Charles Taylor and Robert Bellah and his colleagues[8] attempt to demonstrate the point Karl Marx made in his essay 'On the Jewish Question', namely that to acknowledge human beings as essentially individuals means identifying them as isolated social atoms or hermits and that this is destructive of community life. That there is a richer, much more socially compatible yet still fundamentally individual conception of human life (than what we have inherited from Thomas Hobbes and classical and neo-classical economic science) is largely ignored, perhaps because the goal of such critics is to advance to some form of collectivism, never mind the shape of individualism.[9]

Perhaps the most vocal outcry about classical liberal individualism focuses on problems of community within the framework of this political outlook. Without delving into this matter at length, it needs to be noted that because individuality is central to human nature, classical liberalism is not able to advance some general or universal theory of voluntary community life. Indeed, as Robert Nozick observed,[10] what distinguishes the classical liberal or libertarian political order is its hospitality to numerous experiments in human community life. And, indeed, what we find in a nation such as the United States of America is the presence of innumerable overlapping human communities to which nearly all citizens simultaneously belong. Yet it is arguable that the only human community as such — suitable to any and every human beings — is one that does not impose particular community goals on its citizenry. It makes it legally and otherwise possible, however, to

---

[8] Charles Taylor, 'Atomism', in *Philosophy and the Human Sciences* (Cambridge: Cambridge University Press, 1985); Robert Bellah, *et al.*, *Habits of the Heart, Individualism and Commitment in American Life* (New York: Harper & Row, 1985) and *The Good Society* (New York: Harper & Row, 1991). One might take note, also, of the recent development of organizations, with the leadership of Professor Amitai Etzioni, devoted to the furthering of communitarianism. See the journal published to this end, called *The Responsive Community*, under Professor Etzioni's editorship, as well as his book *The Spirit of Community* (New York: Crown, 1993).

[9] For a detailed discussion of some of the points mentioned above, see Tibor R. Machan, *Capitalism and Individualism, Reframing the Argument for the Free Society* (New York: St. Martin's Press, 1990). In this work I identify what I call 'classical' individualism, so as to distinguish it from the *homo economicus*, neo-Hobbesian version that is the usual target of critics such as Karl Marx, Michel Foucault, Thomas Spragens, Jr., and Amitai Etzioni. See, also, Tibor R. Machan, *Classical Individualism* (London: Routledge, 1998).

[10] Robert Nozick, *Anarchy, State, and Utopia* (New York: Basic Books, 1974), Part III, 'Utopia.'

develop innumerable communities — churches, clubs, neighborhoods, corporations, professional associations, fraternities, political parties, etc., etc. This is just what one would expect in light of the fact of the essential individuality and uniqueness of human beings — that this aspect of their nature be reflected in the variety of communities their interaction generates.

Accordingly, every effort needs to be made by men and women, all of whom at least implicitly set themselves the task of flourishing here on earth, not to allow the backsliding of contemporary culture to become dominant. Such an effort must, however, be made without resorting to any violation of the individualist principles — i.e., without censorship. It must be a matter of relentless argument and application of the principles of individualism to public policies and private conduct.

Unless the momentum is maintained in sustaining the political revolution that has turned human legal institutions toward supporting the flourishing of all human individuals here on earth, there will be massive reversals toward class warfare and oppression. Some signs of those reversals are evident already and the diminished prominence of individualism among American intellectuals and political figures has made the advance of this revolution less likely now than it had been earlier. One can only hope that members of the intelligentsia will not continue be mesmerized by alternative systems that promise them greater powers over others in the name of chimerical politics, culture and economics. Calls for civility and virtue ought not to replace the initiative of human individuals and their voluntary associations with state power. Such calls impede rather than advance the humanistic objectives that impelled the founders of the American republic to put freedom first, as the central public good to which nothing else must be sacrificed.

Utilitarian versus Rights-based Libertarianism

One of the important questions that arise in connection with political economy is how to reason about public policies. When citizens consider how problems are to be solved, they can think in several different ways, but two are prominent and have been the most widely considered live options, at least in Western societies. These are the utilitarian and the rights-based approaches.

Utilitarianism, a form of consequentialism, is the theory of values that urges us to do what will produce the greatest good, as measured by what most people want or desire, or what will satisfy the most of them. For example, whether farmers should receive government subsidies in the form of, say, price supports, is often considered on the basis of whether this will have overall good or bad social results. This approach to decision making derives from the utilitarianism of John Stuart Mill, although since Mill included liberty as an essential part of happiness — or satisfaction or good — today's version of utilitarianism differ from his considerably.

The rights-based approach sets certain principles — for example, natural and thus unalienable rights[11] — as guides to public policies. For example, whether women should be protected from rapists or even stalkers is usually considered on the basis of what their rights are, not whether such protection will have overall social benefits. The rights approach draws on the work of John Locke, although, as with Mill, the current renditions tend to be different in their understanding of human nature and the strictness of, for example, property rights.

In America, as well as in other relatively open societies, there is much debate about whether to respect individual rights regardless of currently estimated consequences, or to ignore those rights if the consequences are deemed to be worth it.

The founding documents of America, and the broad intellectual tradition of classical liberalism from which those documents and their support derives, consider both the general welfare and our unalienable rights (Adam Smith was a type of utilitarian while John Locke was a rights theorist.) Not that these two concerns must be in conflict. Often the best results society-wide come from acting in a principled fashion. But those who champion utilitarianism tend to believe not in principles but in consequences, alone; while rights theorists tend to put the primary emphasis on principles.

Gun Control and Software Control

For example, in the ongoing debate about gun control or the more recent dispute about whether Microsoft Corporation ought to be broken up, even those who hold the same opinion about what ought to be done do not defend that opinion in the same way. Opponents of gun control sometimes say that such measures are too costly and do not produce enough good, so scrap them; or they say that people have the right to bear arms, so no one has the authority to ban or regulate gun ownership whatever the estimated consequences. With regard to the anti-trust suit against Microsoft, some argue that breaking up Microsoft will hurt instead of help more people, so it is a bad idea; others say Microsoft has a right to conduct business so long as it does not engage in force and fraud, and it hasn't done these, so don't break it up, never mind how the public will fare from this.

---

[11] If one has a right because of his nature, then unless one ceases to be what one is, one cannot lose the right, *ergo*, it is unalienable.

Different arguments, same conclusion. So, if we're getting to the same place, why even bother asking whether the rights approach or the consequentialist approach is the correct one?

Well, for someone who cares about the character of politics, not to mention the successful living of life, the issue is crucial. Can principles be identified such that we can stick to them confidently in every context to which they properly apply — or must we consider each case anew, from scratch? Is it not enough to know that we have basic rights as human beings, deriving from our very nature and the requirements of our survival, and then to abide by this knowledge, whether or not *some* of the consequences of respecting those rights turn out to be inconvenient to somebody or other? Or must our individual rights be held hostage to a demonstration of the wider public benefits each time the question comes up, with those rights regarded as expendable if the tally of public benefits looms sufficiently large?

This latter is clearly not a calculation most of us in the USA make when it comes to freedom of expression and religion. We do not try to determine in each case whether the freedom to worship leads to a better religious or general climate, nor whether freedom of expression, especially in the press, produces more good than, say, a government-regulated press. Why? *Because we care about those freedoms so much* — and so we want each individual to enjoy them as a matter of course. We don't want to put those freedoms at risk by letting them be subject to a cost-benefit analysis every time someone publishes a broadside or opens a church. Presumably we have learned that lesson a long time ago and we take it that this lesson has staying power. (Of course, our allegiance to principle even in these realms is not perfect — as witness the speech constraints that our governments impose on broadcasters that they does not impose on print publishers.)

Rights theorists think the same principled approach is valid when it comes to other arenas, including the right to bear arms. Sure, some people will misuse guns and this will have some undesirable, even deadly, consequences. But all in all, respecting the rights of individuals to bear arms ought to be seen as having staying power, too, as an expression of the right of self-defense which is in turn based on the right to life itself. To consistently respect and protect basic individual rights is the best overall course for human beings to take as they live in their communities.

Just a Lot of Flux?

Some see this approach as mistaken because they believe the world is not a steady, stable place at all but rather in constant flux, so that no such principles can be counted on. Even if principles do hold up over time when it comes to scientific realms like physics and chemistry, the same cannot be said of human affairs.

And if principles do not apply in human affairs, to insist that people be honest or generous or just as a matter of principle, rather than on a pragmatic case-by-case basis, makes no sense. We should not even praise integrity, the virtue of upholding one's basic ethical principles in the face of even the greatest of temptations. Keeping promises and honoring oaths, too — even when inconvenient — would be silly. No such consistency could be expected of sensible people. There would certainly be no grounds for assailing, say, the kind of near-continuous lying and promise-breaking we have come to expect from the likes of Bill Clinton.

However, the utilitarian approach to public policy has its own critics. There are many who point out that if there are no reliable principles, then calculating the consequences of policies is itself an impossible and unintelligible endeavor. If there is no rhyme or reason to human life, then all such consequentialist calculations are themselves pointless. Why should we think that breaking up Microsoft is going to be bad for the economy just because similar break-ups had been bad in the past? If, however, there is something we can *learn* form the past, it also follows that we could have learned that, in general, government should not interfere with people's economic affairs. And that would imply that we should respect individual rights as a matter of principle.

The prominent libertarian David Boaz, editor of *The Libertarian Reader*, comments on the matter in an interview in the publication *Full Context*:

> There may be a sense among some Objectivists and other libertarians motivated primarily by concern for individual rights that it's a happy coincidence that pursuing a policy of individual rights leads to the results of prosperity and social harmony, but that if you had to choose, you would choose individual rights over good consequences. That's a false dichotomy. It is implicit, although perhaps not played up as much as it should have been in [e.g. Ayn] Rand's work, that it is not a happy coincidence — it would be unreasonable to expect that the proper philosophy for man did not lead to good results. It would make no sense to demand individual rights for a species for whom the pursuit of individual rights would result in social conflict and poverty. These two lines of argument have to work together.

Of course, most rights theorists such as Ayn Rand and the neo-Objectivists in whose ranks I belong are in some sense consequentialists (or, more precisely, teleologists!) Rights are vital so that we can choose — so that we have the opportunity to choose what is right (but also to run the risk of choosing what is wrong). To the extent that individual rights are protected, every particular individual enjoys the good consequence of being free to act on his own behalf; further good consequences (for himself and others) then depend on how he chooses to act.

The reason for the 'happy coincidence' that respecting rights generates social harmony and prosperity is that when rights are respected, the incentive structure is such that doing wrong tends to hurt oneself, mostly, and the results may not be simply dumped on others. At the same time, one has all the incentive in the world to do productive and beneficial things that are good for others as well as oneself. But there is no guarantee that protecting individual rights will produce, in any given instance, more goodies than some kind of politically coerced or regulated labor might. So when the consequentialists appear to offer such guarantees, they run the serious risk — historically well documented — that if just once they cannot deliver on the promises, argumentatively they will become vulnerable. It was John Maynard Keynes, in fact, who took laissez-faire theorists to task for this, in his little book, *The End of Laissez-Faire* (1927).

Laissez-faire, in short, is no panacea when it comes to secondary consequences, only the best bet!

Honesty is the Best Policy, But Not Always Fruitful

All in all, then, I support the principled or rights approach. In normal contexts, honesty is the best policy, even if at times it does not achieve the desired good results; so is respect for every individual's rights to life, liberty and property. All in all, this is what will ensure the best consequences — in the long run and as a rule.

In which case one need not be very concerned about the most recent estimate of the consequences of banning or not banning guns or breaking up or not breaking up Microsoft or any other public policy, for that matter. It is enough to know that violating the rights of individuals to bear arms is a bad idea, and that history and analysis support this principle. To violate rights has, in the main, produced greater damage than good, so let us not do it even when we are terribly tempted to do so.[12] Let us not do it precisely because to do so would violate the fundamental requirements of human nature. It is those requirements that should be our guide, not some recent empirical data that has no staying power (according its very own theoretical terms).

---

[12] On some occasions one could violate rights and produce greater benefits than without the violation, but it isn't at all clear that this justifies the violation of rights. If, for example, there is special merit in gaining benefits that one chooses to gain, the benefit obtained without having chosen it may be disregarded.

But, finally, you will ask, isn't this being dogmatic? Have we not learned not to bank too much on what we have learned so far, when we also know that learning can always be improved, modified or even revised? Is not progress in the sciences and technology proof that past knowledge always gets overthrown a bit later?

As in science and engineering, so in morality and politics: we must go with what we know but be open to change . . . provided the change is warranted. Simply because some additional gun controls or regulations *might* save lives (*some* lives, perhaps at the expense of other lives), simply because breaking up Microsoft *might* improve the satisfaction of consumers (*some* consumers, perhaps at the expense of the satisfaction of other consumers), is no reason to violate basic rights. Only if and when there are solid, demonstrable reasons to do so should we throw out the old principles and bring on the new principles. And any such reasons would have to speak to the same level of fundamentality and relevance as that incorporated by the theory of individual rights itself.

Those defending consequentialism, like Justice Oliver Wendell Holmes, have argued the opposite thesis: that unless one can prove, beyond doubt, that violating rights in a particular instance is necessarily wrong in the eyes of a 'rational and fair man', the state may go ahead and 'accept the natural outcome of dominant opinion' and violate those rights.[13]

Such is now the leading jurisprudence of the United States of America, a country that inaugurated its political life by declaring to the world that each of us possesses *unalienable* rights, i.e., ones that may never be violated, no matter what!

For reasons made clear in the above discussion, I approach politics via a system of principles — specifically, natural individual human rights, rather than consequentialist or utilitarian arguments. It is not that consequences are not relevant to deciding what political system we ought to support. Only those consequences may be expected to follow from the deployment, both in analysis and the forging of public policy, from the consideration of basic principles based on an up-to-date understanding of human nature.

---

[13] Consider Holmes's dissent in the famous case of *Lochner versus New York* (1905) — in which the Justice archly noted that the Fourteenth Amendment 'does not enact Mr. Herbert Spencer's *Social Statics*' — an opinion that would have more influence than that of the majority.

Chapter 2[1]

Financing Law Without Taxation

Among those who regard liberty as the highest or primary political value, some believe that government is, by its very nature, a morally unacceptable institution.[2]

Others hold, as I do, that government — or what might be more neutrally called the legal authority of the community — is precisely that institution which should be established so as to preserve and protect the liberty accorded to human beings when their fellows refrain from initiating force in human encounters.[3]

Anarchists and statists both believe that government must be coercive. The former hold that therefore no government can be justified, whereas the latter hold that government can be justified because coercion can be justified. But some classical liberals or libertarians reject the view that government *necessarily* entails coercion or the initiation of force (although of course it would entail retaliatory use of force, as against criminals). It is not even the case, some argue, that government must preclude competition from other legal authorities. It only appears to preclude it because the competition is carried out among agencies serving different geographical spheres, much as apartment houses or

---

[1] This essay is a slightly revised version of another of the same title, originally appearing in Tibor R. Machan, ed., *The Libertarian Reader* (Rowman & Littlefield, 1982).

[2] See e.g., Murray N. Rothbard, *Power and Market* (Menlo Park, Calif.: Institute for Humane Studies, 1970). See also his essay 'Society without a State,' in Tibor R. Machan, ed., *The Libertarian Reader* (Rowman and Littlefield, 1982). For a discussion of the anarchism versus limited government controversy, see chapter 3.

[3] I provide a moral case for such a libertarian government in *Human Rights and Human Liberties* (Chicago: Nelson-Hall, 1975) and *Individuals and Their Rights* (LaSalle, IL: Open Court Publishing Company, Inc., 1989).

gated communities compete among themselves ('governing' their own land exclusively but being obliged to keep in mind the options available to tenants and prospective tenants on other plots). And, indeed, there clearly does exist competition for citizens and businesses among countries, and among states or other jurisdiction within countries — even in a context in which the protection of the right to individual liberty is by no means treated as the highest political good.

Those libertarians who believe government can exist without systematically initiating force face some unique problems. Of these I will take up just one: namely, whether it is possible to provide a government — the legal authority of a community — with financial support adequate to its task without relying on any institutional coercive measures such as taxation (i.e., the forcible expropriation of wealth from citizens for purposes of funding the work of governments).

The services provided by governments are commonly regarded as public goods, by which it is meant that such services can be enjoyed even by those who would not choose to pay for them. The most frequently cited example of such a public good is national defense. Once the common defense is secured, everyone can easily benefit from it whether or not he contributed anything to the cost of its production. As John Rawls notes, 'A citizen receives the same protection from foreign invasion regardless of whether he has paid his taxes.'[4] The worry is that if we relied on voluntary support, such public goods might never be produced at all. Too many members of the community might count on a free ride, believing that *their* support of national defense isn't required in order for it to be produced and thus available to them. As Rolf Sartorius observes, if

> [E]ach agree[s] to cooperate contingently upon others doing likewise [then] each reasons that either enough others so agree and the public good thus becomes available to him free of charge, or enough others do not and thus there would have been no point to agreeing in the first place.
>
> Individuals would not voluntarily cooperate toward [the support of government], and observing the principle that no one may be deprived of his property without his consent would prevent the state from compelling him to do so, either by way of compulsory taxation or conscription.[5]

The conclusion facing the non-anarchist (or 'archist') classical liberal or libertarian is that we must either acquiesce in governmental compul-

---

[4] John Rawls, *A Theory of Justice* (Cambridge, Mass.: Harvard University Press, 1971), p. 267.

[5] Rolf Sartorius, 'Limits of Libertarianism,' in R.L. Cunningham, ed., *Liberty and the Rule of Law* (College Station, Texas: Texas A&M University Press, 1979), pp. 92, 122.

sion to pay for such public goods as national defense — or do without such goods altogether. Both alternatives are unacceptable for those libertarians who regard government, in its proper form, as an essential and valuable institution of a human community.

It is worth noting that the problem of public goods — i.e., that there can be so many who plan on free riding that the goods may not be produced at all — does not even exist *as a problem* when we are speaking of other than political matters. Some public goods, so-called, have nothing to do with politics, citizenship, or government. For example, people who walk in 'public' places like malls or train terminals are definitely free riders in their unpaid-for enjoyment of the way others dress or look, yet noone insists that these free riders ought therefore to contribute to the costs of wardrobes and makeup of passing strangers. This is because such benefits are not regarded as essential to the preservation of a free society. If others find it too costly to make themselves good-looking at their own expense, so be it; such neglect neither picks my pocket nor breaks my leg. Similarly, if it should cost too much to produce television signals capable of being received by those not paying for them, they might not get produced; but again, television signals are by no means essential public goods. (And yet, despite the steep expense of that production, television signals have indeed been produced, in abundance, for all non-payers, before and after the advent of cable, thanks to the voluntary payment mechanism of advertising. So even frequent free-ridership need not render a project financially infeasible.) By contrast, national defense and other political values are demonstrably essential for the very survival and functioning of a free society, at least as the non-anarchist classical liberal or libertarian conceives of a free society. This is why the public goods problem must be solved before the classical liberal or libertarian who considers government vital can rest assured that his conception of political life is even possible, let alone preferable, to all others.

To a large extent the public goods/free rider problem grows out of the familiar assumption of contemporary economic theory, namely, that everyone is a utility-maximizing individual motivated solely by the desire to pursue private gains. Assuming that a public good is one that an individual would desire, but only at the minimal expense (of his wealth or time) necessary for its attainment, then any opportunity to become a free rider would be seized. This may not require, according to Mancur Olson, 'the selfish, profit maximizing behavior that economists usually find in the market place . . . [for] even if the member of a large group were to neglect his own interests entirely, he still would not rationally contribute towards the provision of any collective or public good, since his own contribution would not be perceptible.'[6] It seems, however, that this result still requires something akin to the economists' assumption, since without it we can easily imagine some citizens contributing to the provision of the public good as a matter of principle (just as people might, and do, vote as a matter of principle, even if they might readily admit the negligible impact of a single ballot on the outcome). Moreover, we can imagine that recognition and discussion of the public goods problem would spur the members of the group in question, if all were not solely eager to secure for themselves what they value at the lowest cost, to make arrangements to overcome the problem. Indeed, this is what often happens when a group of people decide, say, which restaurant to eat in — some of them, realizing that not everyone's preference can be satisfied, simply withdraw from the discussion. Later, when a check is brought for the entire group, those who had lower priced meals will often agree to divvy up the bill evenly. The value of keeping things going, of fraternity, and of related matters that correspond in some measure to the benefits of public goods, is great enough to forgo the chance of getting the best possible deal on the meal.

Richard Tuck has noted that 'the free-rider problem is not in fact a problem of *political* theory alone — it is merely a particular application of a general logical problem', that of the paradox of the Sorites: 'One stone does not make a heap; but the addition of one stone to something that is not a heap can never transform it into a heap.' Tuck argues that our only recourse is 'to treat minute increments as non-negligible, even though the Sorites argument seems to establish that they ought to be treated as [negligible].' With respect to public goods, Tuck observes that 'universal confidence in (say) stable property ownership or continued personal freedom is desirable; a particular defection from such a universal practice in the interest of local utility would not sap that confidence, though iterated defection would.'[7] And, except on the assumption of narrow selfishness, whereby everyone is obsessed with getting away with a free ride, such iterated defection is not inevitable.

The solution I am proposing for the provision of such public goods as national defense does not, however, hinge on how many members of society would defect just in case they could get away with it. Rather, it hinges on recognition of the fact that the provision of other, nonpublic (but government-provided) goods depends on providing public goods as well. Let me first sketch how this suggestion would solve the problem of government financing.

---

[6] Mancur Olson, *The Logic of Collective Action* (Cambridge, Mass.: Harvard University Press, 1965), p. 64.

[7] Richard Tuck, 'Is there a free-rider problem, and if so, what is it?' in R. Harrison, ed., *Rational Action* (Cambridge, Eng.: Cambridge University Press, 1977), pp. 152-56.

A classical liberal or libertarian government would provide crucial private goods that would make it possible to secure voluntary financing of government. The consumer-citizen would need to pay for this 'private good'. Yet, given that the private good is also a uniquely political good, which can be provided only within the framework of a political/legal institution like government, it would afford the opportunity to simultaneously collect support for the public good that is also required.

For example, the protection of contracts is a private good that government provides at some level of the adjudicatory process in contractual disputes. (Even if a dispute is handled by a private arbitration board, the government/legal framework must be 'waiting in the wings' to assure due process in such matters as arrest, trial, imprisonment, and seizure of property, should the decision of the arbitrators be rejected by one of the parties.) The national defense that government would provide is, of course, the classic public good. But as government provides both goods, payment for the former would also serve to subsidize the latter. Think of how Coca Cola buyers indirectly pay for the overhead and security of the company's bottling plants — even though, were they asked to contribute money *directly* for these purposes, they might well refuse . . . and on standard public goods grounds! Similarly, a person who pays a surcharge on a contract need only care about the fact that his fee ensures access to governmental protections, should he be willfully wronged by the partner to the exchange.

In spelling this proposal out a bit, let us first recall that the justification and need of government arises from the objective value to all members of society of living with others without personal militarization, ad hoc adjudication of disputes, and the general insecurity that goes with lawlessness. Individuals who recognize the value of social life readily acknowledge the value of establishing an agency to provide them with the protection and preservation of their rights in accordance with a system of objective law.[8]

Take contracts, for example. Justly upholding the terms of contract is one legitimate government service. One of the benefits of social life is the possibility of extensive promise-making for a variety of purposes — artistic, commercial, romantic, scientific, educational, recreational, athletic, and so forth. Sometimes relations among human beings are such

---

[8] Perhaps I should say that they *should* and probably will acknowledge the value of such an agency. This brings up the issue of how a government is properly established, something that comprises a crucial feature of the libertarian framework but is beyond the scope of the present essay. But see my 'Human Rights, Feudalism, and Political Change,' in A. Rosebaum, ed., *The Philosophy of Human Rights* (Westport, Conn.: Greenwood Press, 1980), pp. 207-51.

that trust, danger of bad reputation, loss of friendship, etc., do not adequately insure against loss of value, unfairly low return on considerable investment, or outright victimization and injury. Some of these concerns can be handled by insurance agencies. But sometimes, when matters are important and complex — as they often are — satisfaction can be obtained only through legal protection, e.g., against the violation of human rights. Here, it is not simply some service, but some service *aiming at justice*, that is sought. Contracts are one way of insuring against serious loss and supporting efforts towards recovery, but by means that remain attentive to human dignity, that is, to the fact that no one is officially permitted to violate the natural human rights of individuals in the community. Clear terms of contract are generally sufficient to provide the necessary protection, precisely because of the general regard in a society for law and justice. When contracts prove insufficient, government is waiting in the wings.

Government is the institution of a community specifically responsible for maintaining (rights-related) justice among members as members. Frequently, this task can be accomplished only by the use of physical force, which government, adhering to the principles of due process — e.g., stringent rules of evidence, probable cause, speedy and fair trial provisions, etc. — is charged with objectively dispensing.

Promise breakers could have good reason for breaking their contractually stipulated promises, but they would have even better reason to reassure their trading partners about the recovery of investment or avoidance of serious losses in the event a contractual agreement did have to be breached. Thus, even in pure utility-maximizing terms, members of society would ordinarily find it beneficial to secure the private good of government protection and enforcement of contracts (even if government is involved only as the ultimate protector — waiting in the wings). Especially in a human community in which traders do not know each other personally, the prospect of entering into enforceable contractual relationships must be of considerable objective value to practically everyone.

For these and related reasons, the private good of having one's own liberty preserved and protected in the context of contractual relationships would be one of the most widely sought services of government in a free society. Every valid contract imposes a prospective burden on the legal system and its administrators. The 'machinery' for interpreting and enforcing contracts, should disputes arise, must be in place. Providing this protection thus requires ongoing expenditures by the government. A system of contract fees, collected at the time of the signing or registering of contracts from the most simple to the most elaborately corporate — with provisions for further payment in case of special services generated throughout the period of the contractual relationship — would provide funding for this government activity. Even the faintest appreciation of the staggering number of contracts drawn in contemporary societies on just one day would confirm the revenue-obtaining potential of such a surcharge.

Like contract protection, other governmental services are also deliverable to individuals; so fees for the services rendered could be established for them, too. Among such potentially individualized services are securing criminal justice and defending private homes and businesses, or supervising such defense by private security agents so that due process of law is preserved.[9] Not only would it be possible to require payment for particular services rendered, but, if criminal actions are involved, burdens could be distributed in line with the determination of legal responsibility. For example, court costs could be imposed on guilty parties, and criminals could be required to cover other costs, such as police services.

For government to be able to carry out these functions — to stand ready to adjudicate disputes, defend persons and property, issue arrest warrants, seek reparations, impose penalties or imprisonment — it must be stable and secure. Government, in other words, has overhead costs, including those associated with providing for the defense of the system of laws itself. Foreign aggression, usually aimed at the country as a whole, is obviously a threat to this system. Against this possibility a government should protect the community and itself. That is to say, the institution of government must be so constituted that its protection of its own functions is provided for as a necessary means of preserving and protecting the rights of its citizens. Accordingly, its charges for the provision of its various services would reasonably include some amount to cover the cost of defense against foreign aggression.

It might be thought that in this way the principles of a free society, as conceived along classical liberal or libertarian lines, would be breached. First, would not everyone be required to pay for the government's services, whether he wants to or not? Second, would not those who wish to compete for the provision of similar rights-enforcing services be forcibly excluded?

With regard to the fear of reintroducing coercive financing, it must be observed that entering into contractual agreements, for example, is an entirely voluntary matter. Anyone can, literally, simply accept a hand-

---

[9] In some cases, the possibility of differentiating in service delivery may depend on technological developments, although it is more likely that it would simply require willingness to modify standard commercial practices to the services in question. Skeptics may wish to check out the method of customer differentiation devised by a private provider of fire protection. See Robert W. Poole, Jr., 'Fighting Fires for Profit,' *Reason*, May 1976, pp. 6-11.

shake or friendly wink and avoid contracts altogether, just as a couple can avoid marriage vows and simply remain lovers. Yet the existence of a legal system makes possible a protection of terms of agreement that is stronger than mere promise, should one desire this firmer protection. And such private goods, obtainable from government, would reasonably carry the burden of supporting the public good of national defense.

But what about the objection that in a free society government could not legitimately bar others from providing, say, contract protection? Protection that those competitors could then offer at a lower price, inasmuch as they have no national-defense overhead to worry about? In that case, it is argued, government would lose its private-goods customers to the cheaper and more efficient provider, still leaving us with the public goods problem.[10] Back to square one.

This objection, usually advanced by economists with an anarchist classical liberal or libertarian viewpoint, can be met by noting that government is the political institution established and authorized to pursue justice in the social realm. It is a classic natural — though not coercive — monopoly, and must be a monopoly in its capacity as ultimate arbiter if it is to maintain the internal integrity required for administration of justice. The same services provided outside the legal framework would not be as valuable without provisions for due process of law and at least implicit reliance on a 'final authority' which could definitively resolve any persistent dispute, if necessary. In the course of human events disputes often arise and sometimes culminate in conflict; it is beneficial to all for an institution to be in place that can provide for the most peaceful, least-rights-violating procedures necessary to solve the problem. In short, there will very likely be greater demand in the last analysis for *government-backed* arbitration proceedings; the very logic of establishing government (from the ethical point of view of why government *should* be established) would generate this demand.[11]

Outside the context of a classical liberal or libertarian conception of government, this solution might be challenged on grounds, among others, that governmental costs for a welfare state or highly interventionist state are enormous. Indeed, the very existence of deficit spending in most modern societies suggests that not even taxation can secure enough funding for the governments of such states. But our problem is the funding of a constitutionally limited government organized in line with principles of justice. In classical liberal or libertarian theory, the proper scope of government is confined to securing Lockean natural (individual human) rights. Only the preserving and protecting of

---

[10] See, e.g., David Friedman, *The Machinery of Freedom* (New York: Harper & Row, 1973), chapter 34.
[11] Machan, op. cit., *Human Rights and Human Liberties*.

everyone's Lockean rights is the legitimate concern of the government; all its structures, tasks, and mechanisms must serve that end.[12]

Although such a service is a public good that can be made private in its particular delivery (as in the case of contract enforcement), rights protection is still a public good in the sense that its provision is good for members of the community as such, for citizens as citizens. But because there is a definite constraint on what constitutes such a public good, its provision will not involve so much cost as is now commonly associated with governmental operations that range from some bona fide public goods — e.g., criminal law and national defense — to such nonpublic goods as national public radio, mail service, and the printing of money.[13] (Not to mention the costs of regulatory and other activities of government that do not entail the provision of goods of any kind.)

In short, then, competition within a single jurisdiction in providing *ultimate* legal protection and adjudication of contracts would be impossible because this good is not solely an economic but also a political good, the provision of which requires the existence and maintenance of an integrated legal system, including national defense.[14] (There could of course, as already noted, be competition among arbitration services that do still submit themselves to the final legal authority of government.) To prohibit the provision of rights-enforcement that tries to wield authority utterly outside the context of the legal system is tantamount to prohibiting vigilante groups, lynching, and similar extra-legal processes. Such actions always involve third parties whose rights are seriously endangered without the full protection of due process of law.

The fee-for-services-plus-overhead solution is not the only one that could be invoked to finance the administration of governments in a free

---

[12] For the view that libertarian natural rights are not the familiar Lockean rights which impose only negative duties on others — e.g., the obligation to refrain form initiating physical force against others — but that they instead 'involve providing people with positive benefit,' see James W. Nickel, 'Is There a Human Right to Employment?' *Philosophical Forum* 10 (Winter-Summer 1978-79): 164. But this view is mistaken, and the mistake stems from the belief that human rights are rights against government as distinct from rights that should be respected by all and for the protection and preservation of which governments should be established. See my 'Wronging Rights,' *Policy Review* 17 (Summer 1981): pp. 37-58.
[13] I develop the argument for this in 'Rational Choice and Public Affairs,' *Theory and Decision* 12 (September 1980): 229-58.
[14] For more on this see, David Kelley, 'The Necessity of Government,' *The Freeman* 24 (April 1974). None of this precludes the free operations of security services, arbitration groups, etc., which are ultimately accountable to government and do not undertake the enforcement of decisions independently of government.

society. As Ayn Rand has suggested,[15] emergency funds could also be raised through lotteries or even by appealing for contributions, e.g., in a time of war. The integrity of the system would be evident all along, so a genuine threat to the system requiring military action could be demonstrated readily in public debate conducted by a free press, the educational and scientific communities, and so forth. Given the fact that liberal democratic regimes are closest to the policy envisioned by libertarians (and that they have all along received relatively solid popular support), the probability of support for the classical liberal or libertarian system — including extraordinary support in times of trouble — may also be assumed. But what must be stressed is that it is possible to secure the public good of the maintenance of justice, including protection of the citizens from domestic and foreign aggression, without disregarding those very values. (It may be granted that all proposals to secure justice maintenance carry risks of abuse and neglect — if we also grant that the elimination of such risks from human affairs is not only impossible but dangerous to pursue, as the likely casualty of such pursuit would be appropriately limited government itself. Consider, for example, how many proposals for campaign finance reform would entail systematic violation of the right of free speech.)

There is, of course, no guarantee that a government of a classical liberal or libertarian society *would be* voluntarily financed. Spells of neglect could settle in; or there could be periods during which government is not needed, when the world of the anarchist libertarian might be realized, at least briefly.[16] Yet, whenever the challenge is posed to provide such a guarantee, it must be noted that coercive funding of government is hardly a warrant against a government's going bankrupt, waging unsuccessful and unwarranted wars, neglecting its obligations, etc. Richard Tuck observes:

> It has been customary for political theorists to accept that [the free rider-public goods] argument is a good one, and to direct their energies toward devising strategies to cope with it. The most popular has undoubtedly been some mechanism of social coercion, despite the fact that such mechanisms characteristically depend on cooperative action by the people concerned, and that the argument is therefore likely to turn into a *regressus ad infinitum*.[17]

---

[15] Ayn Rand, 'Government Financing in a Free Society,' in E.S. Phelps, ed., *Economic Justice* (Baltimore: Penguin Books, 1973), pp. 363-67.

[16] Certain periods of individualist anarchism are thought to have occurred throughout human history. See, for an example, Joseph R. Peden, 'Property Rights in Celtic Irish Law,' *Journal of Libertarian Studies* 1 (Spring 1977): 81-95.

[17] Tuck, *op. cit.*, 'Free-rider Problem,' pp. 147-48.

If we reject, as we should, the false and impossible ideal of guaranteed provision of public goods, then a solution along the lines sketched above will have to be assessed comparatively.[18] It will have to be judged in accordance with how well it would secure the values members of society *should* seek from a legal system — namely, protection of their basic individual rights.

---

[18] Further details and refinements of this and related tasks of a libertarian political system are, of course, required; but it is usual for those to emerge only after the basic framework proposed is deemed workable. The political science and legal elaboration of libertarianism presuppose the basic plausibility of the general system.

Chapter 3

Private Property Rights

Why *Private* Property?

Let me begin by explaining what I mean by the right to private property and why I use what some now consider an old-fashioned term, abandoned in favor of, say 'the right to several property'.[1] This right is the social-political principle that adult human beings may not be prohibited or prevented by anyone from acquiring, holding and trading (with willing parties) valued items not already owned by others. Such a right is, thus, unalienable[2] and, if in fact justified, is supposed to enjoy respect and legal protection in a just human community.

In the development of classical liberalism there emerged in Western political thought a shift of focus as to the prime unit in social-political matters, from the group — a tribe, class, state or nation — to the human individual. It started with the effort to gradually transfer power from a few or even one person as the source of collective authority and power to more segments of society involved in exercising such authority and power, leading, eventually, to the sovereignty of the human individual. The way power is diffused, when individuals are sovereigns rather than groups, is through the fact that individuals have only a little and highly diversified power to wield. In consequence, they aren't likely to impose themselves on others by, say, starting a war, even when they

---

[1] See, for example, Randy Barnett, *The Structure of Liberty* (London: Oxford University Press, 1998). One reason that it is useful, at least in the context of political philosophy and moral theory, to keep with the terminology of 'the right to private property' is that this right is tied to an important element of classic liberal social and political thought, namely, individualism.

[2] While the right to own may be unalienable, what one owns isn't and may be traded, given away and even destroyed (as Karl Marx was so eager to point out in his essay 'On The Jewish Question', in Karl Marx, *Selected Writings*, ed., D. McLellan [London: Oxford University Press, 1977].).

disagree very seriously. That, in essence, was one of the initial motivations for moving toward individualism, which, when implemented via law and public policy, is much more conducive to peace and, as a result, to prosperity than is any form of collectivism. The liberal order gained support, also, from the conflict between church and state, of course. Indirectly, however, he intention to decentralize power was a major factor here as well. The objective of becoming more productive via the invisible rather than visible hand also contributed to bolstering the case for classical liberal institutions.

Thus classical liberalism has had some considerable support on practical grounds — its usefulness to attaining various widely sought-after objectives. But, one may ask, why would these practical consequences flow from establishing liberal institutions. Why is it better to have a more decentralized polity, an unplanned economy? Why would prosperity come more readily from the invisible rather than the visible hand?

Arguably the answer is that individualism makes better sense than its competitors because the view that *human beings are primarily parts of a social whole* is wrong. This last is a false notion. When invoked, it tends to serve as a disguise for certain special or vested privileges of some members of society.[3] Generalizing such special or vested interests, the values or goals pursued in their name, has been a major source of political acrimony throughout human history. It even continues to drive much of contemporary democratic politics.

There is, however, the problem that as far as its ethical presuppositions and implications are concerned individualism, and in consequences also classical liberalism, have not fared all that well. These views are constantly being charged with opposition to community life and human fellowship, hedonism, materialism, and so forth. Even though this is wrongheaded, without a solid moral case it is difficult to show that to be true. The reason is that morality is extremely important in human affairs. Most people do not confidently embrace a political

---

[3] This is what public choice theory, within contemporary political economy, has helped identify. See, however, Harold Kincaid, *Philosophical Foundations of the Social Sciences: Analyzing Controversies in Social Research* (London: Cambridge University Press, 1996), in which the author argues that the individualist stance in modern economics is mistaken and that we ought to deploy a more holistic approach. Kincaid and many other critics of what they dub 'liberal individualism' claim that individualism is atomistic. While some may, certainly not all individualists fit this description. Nor is that the only version of individualism that gives rise to liberal politics. A good case in point is John Locke, among the early liberals, and many others such as Ayn Rand, Eric Mack, Douglas B. Rasmussen, Douglas J. Den Uyl, Fred D. Miller, Jr., and the late David L. Norton, in our own age.

stance unless it manages to embrace certain basic moral principles. Pragmatic reasons thus never suffice to establish the soundness of political systems and public policies.

It is part of the point of this essay to show that private property rights accord with certain basic moral principles. These are the indispensability of human agency in any sensible moral framework and the moral virtue of prudence. I will argue that individualism embraces these principles and that the right to private property makes their actual realization possible in human community life.

So here the question is 'What is morally right about the institution of private property rights — why it is justifiable to have such laws in a community?' And by this I mean not to focus on such instrumental or pragmatic matters as how useful property law is for purposes of facilitating productivity or wealth or innovation. It may be all that, of course. Yet this essay focuses on the even more crucial issue of whether that institution makes morally good sense or whether critics such as Marx are right to condemn it as a promoter of hedonism, selfishness and greed.

To go about my task with some hope of success I need to begin by saying something about the nature of morality. Basically morality concerns how to live one's life properly, rightly, in a worthy manner, nobly, honorably. To be morally good is to choose to do what will make a person excellent as the kind of being he is, to make one a human being who lives virtuously — honestly, prudently, generously, courageously and so forth.

To live a morally good life amounts to choosing to live so as to fulfill the requirements of one's nature. So our first task will be to take a brief glance at human nature.

Morality, Humanity and Individuality

Since Aristotle spelled it out explicitly, it has been clear enough and difficult to dispute that what makes us all distinctively human is that we have a self-awareness that consists of thinking, of understanding in concepts, and of guiding our conduct by principles, not just by spur-of-the moment feelings, wishes or desires. This is so widely evident in human life and history that, while philosophers like to discuss the nuances, no one can reasonably doubt it. What is less widely acknowledge is that human nature includes, as one of its distinctive features, a significant element of individuality. This is vital because private property rights ties in very closely with human individuality.

A quick indicator of this fact is the thought experiment in which one imagines that if a good friend dies, it is plainly nonsense to believe, 'Oh well, I'll just replace my friend with someone else.' One cannot just replace a person with another if one regards him as he is most basically, not just as some member of a class of people, such as dentists or auto mechanics. (Even with pets it's difficult to replace them because they become sort of humanized around us.)

On the other hand, with a cow, fly, rock and most other things in the world, replacing them is no problem in one sense because they are not important *individually*. They are important in their relationship to other things, whereas in the case of human beings it is everyone's individuality that matters most, especially in those most significant personal or intimate relationships. You fall in love with an individual, not a banker — when you really fall in love, that is. (Some people 'fall in love' with a type, true enough, but there is something perverse about that — it is somewhat sad to hear, 'Well, I love him because he is in uniform or has a big car.')

Even apart from such commonsense observations there is the clear evidence that whenever we consider human beings, we cannot avoid their volitional conduct — actions they choose to bring about on their own.[4] In intellectual discussions this is evident in the fact that we criticize one another about what we think, holding our adversaries directly or indirectly responsible for alleged misjudgments.[5]

It is a reasonable view, then, that human beings are first and foremost individuals who cause much of what they do. Their actions flow from their thinking and their thinking is the sphere in which they are free, self-determined.[6]

Individualism: True and False

Now individualism is associated somewhat uncomfortably with classical liberalism. The reason is that some have overemphasized the element of individuality, making it seem that we are not also members of communities, even of the human race. Such 'atomistic' individualism has made it seem that classical liberalism is tied to a misguided social philosophy. An example of it may be found in the oft-repeated story, by

---

[4] Exceptions are individuals crucially incapacitated. Political theory and law are not devices for dealing with exceptions, however.
[5] I develop much of this throughout Tibor R. Machan, *Classical Individualism, The Supreme Importance of Each Human Being* (London: Routledge, 1998), especially in Chapter 13. 'Individualism and Political Dialogue.' Any kind of professional, including scholarly and intellectual, malpractice alleged in the course of political or other disputes implicitly rests responsibility with the interlocutors, blaming or commanding them for what they ought to or ought not to have done or said.
[6] For more on this, see Edward Pols, *Acts of Our Being* (Boston, MA: University of Massachusetts Press, 1982) and Tibor R. Machan, *Initiative: Human Agency and Society* (Stanford, CA: Hoover Institution Press, 2000).

economists, of Robinson Crusoe. If one models human life on Crusoe's story and his interaction with Friday, it appears that we are born capable of self-sufficient productive conduct and from the start choose whether to associate with others. Yet this idea is patently absurd, considering that all human beings are born helpless and grow up in the company of others on whose support they vitally depend.

Yet it is not true that individualism is necessarily committed to *atomism*. One can fully admit to the communal aspects of human life while insisting that we are essentially individuals, as well. Such a robust, what I have called 'classical' individualism, also stresses the importance of the private realm and insists that all bona fide human communities must adhere to the terms individuals set for themselves.

The crucial individualist ingredient of classical liberal social and political theory stresses not some arid independence or isolation of the individual human being but the fact that everyone can make what in principle can be independent judgments as to the kind of communities suitable to one's membership. Given human nature, the element of choice must be preserved in every suitable human community. This is the source of the classical liberal political principles that demands that the consent of the governed be upheld in public policy as well as personal relations. The criminal nature of murder, assault, kidnapping, rape, robbery, burglary and so forth all make sense in terms of this classical or moderate individualism first found in Aristotle philosophy.[7]

Individuality and Privacy

The gist of individualism is, then, that everyone must consent to being used by another. This is because each is important, valuable in his or her own right. And if an individual is important as such, then there is a sphere that constitutes the individual's realm of sovereignty and others

---

[7] 'To [Aristotle] the Individual is the primary reality, and has the first claim to recognition. In his metaphysics individual things are regarded, not as the mere shadows of the idea, but as independent realities; universal conceptions not as independent substances but as the expression for the common peculiarity of a number of individuals. Similarly in his moral philosophy he transfers the ultimate end of human action and social institutions from the State to the individual, and looks for its attainment in his free self-development. The highest aim of the State consists in the happiness of its citizens.' Eduard Zeller, *Aristotle and the Earlier Peripatetics*, trans. B.F.C. Costelloe and J.H. Muirhead (London: Oxford University Press, 1897), pp. 224-26. This idea is developed further in Fred D. Miller, Jr., *Nature, Justice, and Rights in Aristotle's Politics* (Oxford: Clarendon Press, 1995). The difference between the atomistic and classical type of individualism is discussed in Tibor R. Machan, *Capitalism and Individualism, Reframing the Argument for the Free Society* (New York: St. Martin's Press, 1990).

ought to respect it, the realm within which one must make effective judgments about one's life. And indeed in classical liberal, political, and legal theory there's a great deal of emphasis on individual rights rather than rights of families or other groups, bearing on this individualist element of the position. The right to private property is, in turn, the most practically relevant of those individual rights.

The term 'privacy', then, underlines this emphasis of the importance of individuals. The right to private property is really just an extension, within the framework of a naturalist world view, of the right to one's own life. It is when one('s life) engages with the rest of the world in the unique way one will do so, and when another will do this in his or her unique way, then privacy becomes important.[8] It will then be possible to actualize and to protect who one is and one's manifestation in the world — one's own art, productivity, creativity, innovation and so forth. None of those, as well, may be used by others without the individual's consent to whom they belong.

Socialism and Humanity

Now consider that one of the interesting things about socialism is that in deep-seeded socialist theory there are no individuals. Marx said it directly: 'The human essence is the true collectivity of man.'[9] He also noted that human beings constitute specie-beings and comprise 'an organic whole' in the collectivity we call humanity.[10] What is important about you and me for a consistent, thoroughgoing socialist is that we belong to the human race, somewhat analogously to the way a bee

---

[8] A very important beginning had been made on this line of analysis by William of Ockham who regarded property rights as securing 'the power of rights reason', that is, a sphere of personal jurisdiction that made reasoning about what one ought to do possible. This was extended more elaborate in John Locke's idea that one has the right to one's person and estate, something that, if protected, makes choice among other persons possible. An even greater advance on the precise identification of the nature of private property had been made in James Sadowsky, 'Private Property and Collective Ownership', in Tibor R. Machan, *The Libertarian Alternative* (Chicago: Nelson Hall, 1974). Karl Marx, too, got it nearly right when he wrote that 'the right of man to property is the right to enjoy his possessions and dispose of the same arbitrarily without regard for other men, independently, from society, the right of selfishness.' Karl Marx, 'On The Jewish Question', in Robert C. Trucker, ed., *The Marx-Engels Reader* (New York: W.W. Norton, 1978), p. 26. Only, Marx's warped view of human nature prompted him to consider only the most wasteful and pointless way the right to private property might be exercised.

[9] Op. cit., Karl Marx, *Selected Writings*, p. 126.

[10] Karl Marx, *Grundrisse*, trans. D. McLennan (New York: Harper Torchbooks, 1971), p. 39.

belongs to its hive or an ant to its colony, only in this case the constituent parts are intelligent persons.

This is especially true of international socialism, but National Socialism and even more restrictive, local forms of socialism, emphasize the group as a whole and *its* plan, telos or destiny. Even communitarians, as vague as their conception of a community comes to (so that one cannot pin them down as socialists because they leave room for some elements of individualism), speak mostly of concerns on behalf of 'us' and use the term 'we' to designate the primarily valued party when discussing public policy. The individual can then, at times, be sacrificed if some gains are made for the group, collective or community.

Classical Liberalism, Human Nature & Individuality

Yet, if we examine human life carefully, we notice clearly that there is something irreducibly, inescapably, individual about everybody. Just think about yourself. How do you insist on being regarded by friends and others close to you? As a student? An American or Rumanian or Hispanic? Or as a woman or basketball player? Is there not in fact something unique that is the *you* that captures who you are? One's *identity* isn't racial, ethnic, religious or even professional. It is individual. As John Quincy Adams said in the motion picture *Amistad*, ask not *what* someone is but *who* someone is, is to come to know the person.

It's in classical liberalism that this is acknowledged more than in any other political philosophy. There's always been a little bit of emphasis on individuality, of course, in various rebellious political movements, but it's very difficult to maintain the supremacy of the tribe or, later, the state if one admits that what is truly important in a human society is the individuals who comprise it, as individuals. Because then one can not reasonably say, 'Well, we can do away with that individual or with that group of individuals or their projects so as to benefit some others, including some collective such as the state, community, culture or race.'

Indeed, with the recognition and acknowledgment of the supreme value of the individual, the very definition of a 'good' or 'just' society would have to emphasize the freedom and happiness of individuals.

In fact, a characteristic of the classical liberal political ethos is that one scrutinizes a society for its quality, its goodness, and its justice on the basis of how loyal it is to the mission of securing the rights of individuals to their liberty and pursuit of happiness. This is actually a very prominent movement in the world today. It is not done consistently and purely, but all those human rights organizations that go from country to country to check whether they adhere to tenets of justice are at least rhetorically committed to the examination of whether the legal authorities treat human beings who live in their jurisdiction as individuals who have basic rights. Are their projects respected or are they neglected and treated with callous disregard for their individual choices?

This is one of the reasons that in a largely liberal — or, for the sake of avoiding confusion with American liberalism, a classical liberal or libertarian — society membership in a class loses its moral and political significance. In the United States of America, for example, there are matters that may make no difference to most people, but when they matter to even just one, it is appreciated. I, for one, once worked as a busboy in Cleveland, Ohio, and noticed that when paid, I could go back to the same restaurant and eat a meal there. There was no frowning and shaking of the head and saying, 'Wait a minute, you do not belong here'. In much of Europe, in contrast, if you work in a restaurant you do not get to eat there — it is not illegal now but it is certainly gauche.

Fluctuating Classes

In a more or less classical liberal or libertarian social-political society the divisions that are based on incidental attributes — one's wealth, color, national origin, ethnicity, race, and so forth — tend to be less significant because one's individual worth trumps all these and classes, at any rate, are always in a flux. Even racial and ethnic, not to mention religious or economic categories tend to shift because there is no widespread and well-entrenched legally enforced barriers to either entry to or exit from any of them.

Such categories and the behavior associated with them may still prevail in certain special contexts. For example, a professor will usually attain special respect in the classroom, but when one meets the professor at a restaurant, one will not need to carry over the behavior associated with that classroom status. No 'Herr Doktor', as, for example, in much of Germany, in or outside the classroom. In most American schools, by contrast, one says, 'Hello Professor', but outside, the label is not usually used.

All this can be a bit disturbing because it can sometimes spill over into disrespect for people who in fact deserve respect. Rampant individualism can corrupt into disrespect for all authority. The corruption can, but by no means need, be generated by the notion that individuals matter primarily as individuals, not so much as members of classes. It is also evident enough that we are social beings, members of the class of human beings, and there are some matters very important about that, too.

The Moral Standing of Private Property Rights

Individualism does, however, underlie the regime of private property rights. But why do we need a separate discussion of the merits of the right to private property? What will such an inquiry yield?

There are at least two answers to that question. One is that when you resist people taking something from you, by taxation, theft or any other means, it is important to know, even if only implicitly, that the resistance is justified. That it is a kind of self-defense, akin to resisting someone assaulting or raping someone else. It is vital to learn that one is in the right and is not doing something merely willful or stubborn or prejudicial, that one is not just being a recalcitrant, antisocial person, when one insists on the integrity of ownership. This is a point widely contested by opponents of classical liberal or libertarian legal orders.

When all things are considered, the most important questions about liberalism and its various tenets is, 'Is it true?' 'Is classical liberalism or, its purest versions, libertarianism, the way a society ought to be organized?' And, in order to answer that question, one must examine whether its various tenets can withstand challenges, criticisms and so on. Individualism is one of these tenets but the right to private property is the most important practical, public policy element of it.

The second reason we need to examine private property rights is whether the system of individual rights, including the right to private property, is a just system? Or is it, as many critics claim, just a figment of some people's imagination?

One of the most prominent and oft-repeated criticisms leveled at classical liberalism, especially by students of various configurations of Marxism — there are about 300 versions now — is that this whole emphasis on individuality is a kind of historical glitch. It is only a temporary phase in history which had its role but now can be dispensed with.

Individualism and Historicism

The Marxists and many others, some who follow them without knowing it, claim that in the sixteenth century the individual was *invented*, not merely discovered or his existence politically affirmed, for the sake of sustaining economic productivity. In order to create motivation for wealth-creation, the individual had to be made seem significant. It is a myth, but it is a useful myth. It is like telling someone that she is beautiful when she isn't so that she will do certain things from which certain advantages derive.

According to Marxists, there was a period of human history where the belief in the importance of the individual had an objective historical function, not because it was true, but because it contributed to certain crucial elements of capitalism.

There are people who look at history in this way, as if it is the record of the growth of humanity from infancy to full maturity. They then take it that the bourgeois epoch is like the adolescence of an individual. It is a temporary stage and has its usefulness because, typically, adolescents embark upon all sorts of useless ventures as a sort of exercise to prepare for adulthood. It trains them for the eventual serious challenges of maturity.

When one treats humanity this way, so that it has these various historical stages, individualism can be regarded as one of those stages. It's a somewhat appealing picture — it fits some images we have of humankind. Ecologists encourage this, as do some moral visionaries who see humanity as a big family or some other kind of collectivity.

Marx explicitly said that the Greek era was the childhood of humanity. He, as I have noted already, and many of those who have been influenced by his thinking, believe that humanity is some kind of organism — a being of which individuals are the parts. Humanity goes through stages of organic development, tribalism its first and communism its final stage. And while the individualist stage in a necessary one, it is certainly not the completed stage of humanity.

Individualist Alternative to Organicism

These challenges have to be answered because they are extremely well developed, plausible enough, and with enormous influence in the world intellectual community. It is a little like when one meets a friend and asks them to explain some event such as their recent divorce and they proceed to give you a very well worked out and sincerely held rationalization as to how things happened. Now, in order to cope with one of these rationalizations, one must get to the heart of the actual situation and demonstrate beyond all reasonable doubt that the story is a different one. One must show that one's understanding of what's going on is more rational, coherent, comprehensive, and explains much more than does theirs. Otherwise the deceptive story will be the only viable account making the rounds, despite its conflict with common sense.

Unless liberalism is able to identify a better story than what those who champion the organic view advance, it will be defeated, at least theoretically. And while that is not always decisive, it certainly has an impact on the confidence with which the position can be supported and implemented.

Indeed, one of the advantages of anti-liberal doctrines is that so many intellectuals are enchanted by them. They create elaborate and smart stories around them, stories that are extremely appealing and intellectually challenging. For one, such a story gives the intellectual a privileged position. Only intellectuals are in the position to grasp such a complex story, after all. Common sense does not support it. (For example, Marx thought only communists could really understand the truth of such a story, the rest of us having been blinded by our class outlook.)

The Appeal of Collectivism

The idea, for example, that we are all mere parts of a large human organism, humanity, has very a strong intellectual standing in our time. A great many people make reference to humanity — as when they talk about sacrificing oneself or one's private interests or one's materialistic goals for humanity. And others refer to smaller groups — the community or ethnic group or the race — as the organisms that are of significance.

So it is almost a feature of the mainstream to think of us not as individuals but as parts of some larger whole. 'Do you not have something more important to live for than yourself?' 'Is there not something greater than yourself to which your life must be devoted for it to be worthwhile?' Less loosely, some, such as the philosopher Charles Taylor, argue that we all must *belong* to a group, by dint of our very humanity, our nature as human beings. He tells us that 'Theories which assert the primacy of rights are those which take as the fundamental, or at least a fundamental, principle of their political theory the ascription of certain rights to individuals which deny the same status to a principle of belonging or obligation, that is a principle which states our obligation as men to belong to or sustain society, or a society of a certain type, or to obey authority or an authority of a certain type.'[11] Never mind that Taylor cannot give us any such theories — John Locke, for example, rested basic human rights on ethics or natural law. What is important in what Taylor says is not only that if you just live to make the most of *your* life, you are not really living a *significant enough* life. A significant life must fulfill a greater purpose and humanity's purpose is one of the candidates. God's purpose is another candidate. Ecologists have a biological purpose in mind. A significant life must belong to the effort to pursue this purpose and thus our lives, to be properly significant, may be subordinated, by force, to such purposes.[12]

---

[11] Charles Taylor, *Philosophy and the Human Sciences* (London: Cambridge University Press, 1985), p. 188.
[12] The concept 'belong' can be used to refer to membership as well as to being a part of. Membership in human communities embarking on various purposes can be voluntary but being a part of is something ontologically pregnant — one is part of something sometimes whether one likes it or not.

There's a very prominent tradition of selecting alternative wholes larger than ourselves as the proposed beneficiaries of significant human actions. And this can lead to the whole process of forcing individuals to be used for purposes to which they do not consent. This is the greatest source of coercive thinking in human history. Once it is accepted that human individuals are part of a larger whole they, as members of a partnership or team, have enforceable obligations to the goals of that large whole. They belong to it.*

Consider, to appreciate this, how in certain cases we treat such wholes as ourselves. If something happens to one's ear, for example, and yet one prizes one's appearance with an intact ear, then one takes another part of one's body that is not visible and takes part of it so as to replace the ear. The famous Welsh actor, Richard Harris, had his nose destroyed in a fight, so doctors took a part of his hip bone and replaced it, clearly because the nose was more important to an actor than that little part of the hip bone.

Well, if humanity is the larger organism, then maybe a given individual may not be so important a part of it as another. So the less important individual can be sacrificed for the more important one (or the goals of the less important can be sacrificed for those of the more important). One may be an eye and the other just a useless thumb. That picture is widely embraced because of the belief that humanity is some organic whole.

If one recognizes collectivism as a misguided picture of human life, one must carefully and effectively argue in response to these well worked out and often honestly and sincerely meant doctrines. One must demonstrate that it is indeed individuals who count for the most in the human picture. It needs to be proven, some of the widespread opinion to the contrary notwithstanding, that notions such as 'individual rights' are universal and not stuck to some limited historical epoch.

The Right to Private Property

One reason that it must be shown that the social regulative principle of a right to private property is sound and that it ought to be respected and protected in human community life is that it is a vital conceptual or logical implication of the individualist story. If individualism is indeed sound, so is the principle of private property rights. When the right to private property is not respected and not sufficiently protected, then there is something wrong with a community.

---

* Taylor seems clearly to mean by 'belong' 'being part of', so that one can be compelled to adhere to the purpose at hand.

This means that it is not quite fit for human inhabitation, given the individuality of every person and how respect for this is a precondition for his or her flourishing.

There are many different ways in which private property has been supported in the history of political economy. Most prominent has been the claim that there should be legal protection of the right to private property because this facilitates productivity — a point that's in agreement with Marx, only universalized beyond a given epoch. Protecting this right helps society get rich — not only in the 16th century but always. Both Adam Smith and John Stuart Mill tended to argue along these lines: It's a good thing to have these rights because if we act in terms of them we will have greater prosperity. Many economists today argue a similar point. Indeed, that is one reason many governments engage in privatization, so as to encourage economic growth.

All of this is vital but it is not what is most important. What needs to be shown is that the individual has these rights regardless of what's done when simply exercising them. Even if individuals waste away their lives, they have that right. It is theirs to waste away, not someone else's, because they are the important element of society, not some outsider, not some other being such as society, the community, the tribe or the ethnic group. It is this element of liberty, the right to choose how one lives, that is most central to human community life, even if, indeed because, as a matter of one's personal life it is equally important to make the right choice, to choose to do the right thing.

That is exactly why the right to private property is vital. When effectively protected, it secures for human individuals a sphere of personal jurisdiction, the right to acquire and hold the props, as it where, with which to order one's life. Moral virtues such as generosity, kindness, courage, moderation, prudence and the rest are all imperatives the practices of which engage one with the natural world as humans best can do so. If one is not in charge of some of that world one cannot conduct oneself virtuously. So the right to one's life, liberty and property are necessary conditions for a morally significant or meaningful life in human communities.

It needs to be noted here, as a significant aside, that even if we are essentially individuals, this doesn't mean we are not also naturally members of societies. But, as moral agents and as candidates for membership in some human communities or societies, we are morally responsible to take into consideration and never neglect the fact that we must judge those societies as to whether they do adequate justice to our individuality, most generally, and whether they best serve our flourishing.

Assigning Property

Perhaps the most troublesome aspect of the right to private property is how it is to be established that some item belongs to someone. In a complicated modern society wherein the system of private property rights enjoys legal standing, assigning particular items — a vehicle, house, parcel of land, tree, computer, song, musical arrangement or anything else that could be owned — to someone is a matter of common law practices. Titles are initially obtained to parcels of land, at least ideally, by means of someone making a claim of ownership or by someone having taken part in an exchange of money for land.

Yet for purposes of political philosophy and economy, this isn't sufficient to show that assignments of ownership can be justified. Such claims as that everyone's ownership goes back in history to some instance of conquest or theft cannot be met merely by noting that today the system is manageable, especially when it is the system itself that is being challenged on grounds that there is something unjust about all original and subsequent acquisition. Since, however, none of us were present when such acquisition occurred — or only in rare cases would such acquisition have occurred in a past that's familiar to us — only a method of rational reconstruction is available to us, via thought experiments that show that such acquisition could have been just.

Arguably, then, we need to imagine first acquisitions that are morally unobjectionable. For example, a human being may have at one time sought to cultivate land and came upon a parcel suited to his or her purposes that hadn't yet been claimed by anyone. So, the individual or the family made the decision to lay claim to the parcel of land and fenced it off so as not to have others disturb the fulfillment of the intended purpose. Henceforth this parcel belonged, rightfully, to the individual or family making such a decision. If later others arrived, they would learn, from the prior arrival and decision of the first arrival(s) and their subsequent use of the parcel in question, that it is no longer available for them without violently taking it. Such scenes are quite plausible and their moral propriety can also be shown to a reasonable degree of plausibility. After all, to embark upon the claim to and subsequent use of the parcel of land in question is something the individual or family involved ought to do, as a matter of prudence or good sense, of making sure that a livelihood is secured and plans to sustain it can be made. If some danger from others might be in the offing, it would also make sense to perhaps employ the services of some persons with special fighting skills to rebuff any efforts by others to take the parcel from the owners. And, in light of the awareness that some claims to parcels of land could be contested, the setting up of forums of dispute resolution would also make sense, with specialists to carry out the enforcement of the resolution of disputes.

Now this calls forth the issue of whether any kind of absolute rights to private property could be expected to be in force when these kinds of events commence among human beings. Yet, this is not as difficult a matter to contemplate as some make out. Although no a priori or deductive system of decision-making can be expected to function in these sorts of cases, it is not difficult to envision that when the dispute resolution process commences, those familiar with the circumstances and people involved will have the needed information to reach a solution that should be binding on all. Such a resolution would amount to a decision by, say, a court, after the required deliberation, as to who owns what. After such a decision is made, beyond a reasonable doubt about it, those to whom the parcels of land are thus assigned can be said to have an incontestable right to this land. That's as absolute as we can expect, which is absolute enough, when contrasted to ongoing common 'ownership' that fosters interminable tragedies — tragedies of the commons from several points of concern.

No *Carte Blanche* to Communities

From this it follows that we must always keep in focus the question of whether we ought to live in a given community. Do we — ought we to — want to support this kind of public policy, this kind of a legal system? What is the standard by which we make that kind of decision when we have the chance? The issue of what principles should govern human communities lie at the most basic level. The right to private property is one of those principles.

Very often we don't have a direct practical option to act on the choice we make about basic principles. But at least we can think about them so that when we do get a chance to make a significant decision, then we will know where to stand. We owe it to ourselves, to a life of integrity, not to forget about that issue, ever. That is the highest duty of citizenship!

Property Rights, Individuality and the Moral Life

So what does the right to private property do in connection with the essential human element of individuality?

Well, as already suggested, the right to private property secures for one a sphere of sovereignty. If we are individuals, required, morally, to lead our lives by our judgements, it is crucial that we control the elements with which our lives are lived. Indeed, it becomes the most crucial thing.

The question, 'How ought I to live?' becomes the foremost question to which you then seek an answer. While most of us aren't moral theoreticians or ethical philosophers, that question still is always near the forefront of our minds. No matter what you do, even reading these lines, the question will arise: 'Should I sleep or should I pay attention? Should I consider this point or should I just glide over it?'

All of those are questions having to do with your ethical agency, with one's governance of one's life, with one's sovereignty. One's feeling that one is doing the right thing becomes crucial if one is indeed the master of one's existence.

Now, without the right to private property, without having some props, some elements of reality that are under our jurisdiction, our ethical decisions cannot be effectual. Consider, for example, if it turns out to be true that a good human being ought to be generous. Well, if we do not have the right to private property how are we going to be generous? Are we going to be like politicians and bureaucrats and expropriate what belongs to others and give this to the poor and needy? That's not generosity. That's theft.

In short, then, in order to have a effective life of moral virtue, for example the virtue of generosity, we must have the right to property, to hold and then to be free to part with valuables, on your own terms.

Moral Individualism

Although collectivism has some currency, especially among intellectuals and social theorists, so does a particular version of individualism. I have in mind the sort that pertains to moral responsibility.

Few people ever quite let go of the idea that some things they and others do are good and some things bad and that those doing them are responsible. When others judge our lives, or when we reflect upon ours, we say, 'I did or did not do the right thing.' Moreover, we can go on to consider what we did with what belongs to us — to use it well or badly.

Without our sphere of sovereignty, that is manifest in the actual world where we live our lives, we would not be able to act on most moral principles, especially those that involve allocating resources. Are we stingy? But one has to be stingy with something. If one is a neat person, one has to be neat within some sphere that one keeps orderly. If a slob, one will need something that belongs to one that one isn't taking good care of. If those items don't belong to you, if you always have to ask permission of society or the clan or the tribe of the nation as to what to do with these things, the you are not the effective agents in the disposition of them. And you are then not an effective moral agent either. You cannot take pride in what you achieve, nor feel guilt for your failings. You are basically just a little bit of a cell in this larger organism.

The Virtue of Prudence

Prudence is one of the virtues identified in classical Greece. I want now to discuss it in a little more detail than thus far.

First, in the modern era prudence has been demeaned because the task of taking care of oneself and one's own has been deemed to be instinctual ever since Thomas Hobbes argued that we are all driven to preserve ourselves. But Hobbes rested his case on extrapolating the principles of classical mechanistic physics to human life, a move that is not at all justified. Human beings must choose their conduct, including whether they will serve others' or their own well-being. Prudence, as the ancients saw it, is the virtue one needs to take decent care of oneself.

Later Immanuel Kant argued that since prudence is a motivation that is aligned to one's own interest or inclinations, it is not a moral virtue. Only motives that are totally indifferent as to one's own interest or inclinations can have moral significance, even though we cannot know whether we are ever so purely motivated.

Neither Hobbes nor Kant had it right. Prudence is a moral virtue, though not the only or highest on. In any case, a prudent person acts, among other ways, economically. Such a person realizes that one must reserve for the future, put resources away for a rainy day. Such a person isn't reckless in the disposition of the resources over which he or she has control.

But now if we have no right to acquire or hold things then we cannot be prudent. We then don't have the decision-making authority to allocate resources in accordance with standards of prudence. On the other hand, if we do have this authority, then we can choose to act prudently.

Prudence and Justice

If in fact it is a moral virtue to be prudent, but it is politically impossible for one to act on that virtue, then there is a basic conflict between ethics and politics. Then the political sphere is not properly *adjusted* to the ethical sphere. Then our ethical agency has not been done sufficient justice by the legal system in which we act.

And, indeed, that is one of the things that is so frustrating in societies where one does not have the right to private property. Not only that one is going to be thwarted in one's efforts to acquire life's necessities, but that one cannot act responsibly. Here what happens is a version of the tragedy of commons.

The tragedy of commons is a problem usually associated with managing the environment. The reason is that most spheres where there are environmental problems are public. The atmosphere, oceans, rivers, large forests and so on are spheres wherein no one is individually responsible. To put it another way, everyone is responsible for the management of such spheres but no one has a clear idea what to do about this responsibility because the limits imposed by private property rights are missing.

When you have a distinct or definite sphere of jurisdiction, however complicated it may be — with various layers of responsibility and delegation — then when something is done wrong, it can be traced to the agent or agents who did it. And when things are done right, again it can be traced to the agent or agents whose responsibility it was to do them right. Without the right to private property this is impossible.

This is one of the reasons that no society can completely abolish private property. It is impossible to act in any sort of responsible way without some sphere of personal jurisdiction.

Moral Responsibility and Private Property

So the right to private property is the concrete manifestation of the possibility of responsible conduct in a community where there are lots of people who need to know what they ought to do and with what they ought to do it. We are talking about a life lived within the context of the natural world. If our bodies are non-existent and we are just living in an illusionary material world, then these matters are of no significance. There is an assumption underlying the right to private property, and indeed many other elements of classical liberalism or libertarianism, namely, that we have a task to live properly in the midst of a natural environment, a natural world. We are not just living a purely immaterial life. Food needs to be grown and distributed; production has to occur. All sorts of concrete, natural tasks need to be carried out in order to facilitate our human lives.

If this natural life turns out to be either illusionary or insignificant, then some of these things loose their importance. Then politics might indeed be subject to different principles, ones that facilitate different goals, different aims from prosperity, flourishing, or other kinds of earthly success. It's not easy to imagine what that would be. Yet, in a philosophical discussion of these issues, one has to contend with the fact that there are alternative basic ideas that are proposed concerning the basic elements of human living. Liberalism has to stand the test of being compared with these alternative pictures.

Naturalism and Politics

The naturalist approach, in the sense we are preparing and forging ways of living within the natural world, is, I am convinced, demonstrably sound. The alternatives tend to be very vaguely and confusedly supported.

There are doctrines in the world that say that all individuality, for example, is a myth. There are Eastern religions that contend that the natural, individual self is an illusion and that in truth, we're all just part of the universal consciousness.

In order to test this, one has to have some criteria by which truth needs to be determined. The naturalist approach rests on the application of criteria that are universally accessible, available to all human beings with their rational faculties intact.

Commerce and Property

Private property rights, of course, sustain the institution of commerce. If you trade goods and services, if you sell them, if you produce them, if you hoard them, if you save them, you have to have some level of jurisdiction over them. If I wanted to trade you my watch for your shirt, then it has to be my watch. Or I have to have delegated to me the authority of someone whose watch it is. And it has to be your shirt; otherwise there would be no ability or justification in engaging in this trade. I can't sell you something that belongs to another. And if it belongs to everyone all at once, no one can sell or trade it and chaos prevails as regards to its use. So commerce, as well as charity and generosity presuppose the institution of private property rights. Without that institution, these activities cannot be undertaken smoothly, without confusion.

Moral Standing of Political-Economic Systems

One of the questions that arise in the discussion of political philosophy and political economy is whether they have moral standing. When the Left criticizes classical liberals morally because the liberal or libertarian polity makes profit-making possible, what is the answer?

It is not enough to just say, 'Well, we just like to make profit.' A murderer can just say, 'We just like to kill people.' That is no justification, clearly.

There are those who argue that a social science such as economics requires nothing from morality — indeed, it is entirely amoral, purely positive or descriptive in its central thrust. But this is a mistake. All human affairs, including economic ones, are permeated with moral issues. In economics, for example, there is the moral (or as Rasmussen and Den Uyl have called it, the meta-normative)[13] element of private property rights.

If one does not own anything, no trade can ensue and all the talk of supply and demand must be abandoned in favor of what collectivists

[13] Douglas B. Rasmussen and Douglas J. Den Uyl, *Liberty and Nature* (Chicago, IL: Open Court Publishing Co., Inc., 1990).

tend to support, a sort of share-and-share alike 'economy.' But to own something means to be in a distinctively normative relationship with others. They are prohibited from taking what belongs to one. They ought not do so and will be penalized, furthermore, if they do.

So the amoral stance on the market economy is doomed to failure. What is needed is a moral or other normative justification of the institution of private property rights.[14]

To do that we must analyze human nature as it is manifest in the natural world. Will such an analysis support the institutions of freedom and free markets and give them a stronger moral standing in human society than alternative ones possess?

Morality and Public Affairs

Now there are some who would dismiss all this because there are cases in human community affairs involving innocent helpless persons, who meet with natural disaster and may find themselves without any voluntary help when they need it. And that is certain a possibility, even if not a likelihood in a free society. James Sterba, for example, has been arguing for decades that because such cases are possible, the people who find themselves in them have a right to welfare that the legal order may protect. These positive rights, whereby others are required to work for such persons — or part with goods they have worked for in order to support them — come about because it would not be reasonable, Sterba argues, to demand that such people respect private property rights. It would be more reasonable to expect of them to strive to obtain the goods they need — ones Sterba calls, in a question-begging fashion, surplus wealth. (As if someone is justified in identifying what constitutes surplus — a term from classical Marxism that makes no sense outside the Marxist framework.)

If one recognizes, however, that an individual's life is his or her own and he or she does not belong to anything or anyone outside of memberships to which he or she consents, then even the most dire needs of others does not support any institutional arrangement that fails to recognize individual rights — to life, liberty, and, yes, property (that one comes by without violating the rights of others even if one does not strictly deserve the property for some kind of service rendered or other achievement — for instance, come by because others want to purchase some talent or other attribute one naturally has). Just as it is unjustified to use others as a shield against natural danger, regardless of how little use one may make of them, one may not use others against their will, including wealth they own. One must find ways around this prohibi-

[14] For more on this, see Tibor R. Machan, 'The Normative Basis of Economic Science', *Economic Affairs*, Vol. 18 (June 1998), pp. 43-46.

tion, as indeed most do when they engage in trade rather than theft in the effort to acquire their own wealth.

It is reasonable to demand this of everyone, even those in dire straits. If, however, in desperate circumstances such people do not honor this prohibition, there can be some measure of forgiveness, even within the purview of the legal authority (as per some cases that have been subject to unusual judicial discretion). But such exceptions, as hard cases in general, make bad general law.

Law and Common Sense

Let me go back to where we started. When somebody robs another who resists, the latter has a common sense idea of doing the right thing — the resistance is not merely some immature, capricious and willful conduct. It is not as if one were simply engaged in feet stomping and crying, 'I want it! I want it! I want it!' No, one can sense that there is right on one's side, not just an arbitrary wish and desire.

That is one reason it is vital to consider whether the free system can be given justification. What has been said here is by no means a thorough defense of the right to private property, but it does furnish some hints as to how such a defense would have to be presented if the issue ever arises, which is quite often in our world. First, this right, if protected, preserves one's moral agency in this natural world in which community life occurs. Furthermore, it punctuates the fact that striving to prosper is a morally valid goal for human beings. So, the moral virtue of prudence, of taking the requisite actions to care for oneself and one's intimates, supports the right to private property as well.

One thing that respect and protection of private property rights makes possible is the pursuit of wealth. Oddly, however, that is a *criticism* many offer against the system of free market capitalism that is built on the legal infrastructure of private property rights. They say, as we have already seen Marx do, that private property rights — if they are protected, maintained, developed as law — encourage a hedonistic, narrowly selfish life, one that is concerned exclusively with acquisition of worldly goods. As he said, 'the right of man to property is the ... right of selfishness.' Freedom is supposed to make too much self-indulgence, including pleasure, possible.

So another question that arises here turns out to be, 'Is pleasure justified?' For even if the right to private property could be used for purposes quite different from obtaining pleasure in life, if pleasure is something loathsome and this right somehow encourages its relentless pursuit, perhaps it is an institution that is more harmful than benign.

We cannot enter this topic at length but this much should suffice for now. If we are indeed natural beings in this world, one of our important values will be pleasure, the good feelings we experience *via* our bodies. This is so even if there are higher goods, the attainment of which may require giving up some pleasure.

So now, if wealth brings with it the possibility of pleasure, then wealth itself is a worthy good, provided it is not stolen but created, produced, and that it is not chosen as the highest good if a higher one can also be identified.

Abandoning the Divided Self Idea

If one has a completely different view of human nature, whereby only the spiritual side of human life is of significance, then one will embrace a different system of values and probably also champion different institutions. We have a powerful tradition in most civilizations whereby there is an uneasiness about facilitating the flourishing of the human body. And that is often what stands, at a most basic level, against the free society!

One reason underlying that stand is the lack of a clear, unambiguous and benign acceptance of our earthly selves. We often think ourselves to be so unique, so extraordinary that we believe we must be partly divine or otherworldly. St. Augustine said it well when he cried out, 'How great, my God, is this force of memory, how exceedingly great! It is like a vast and boundless subterranean shrine ... Yet this is a faculty of my mind and belongs to my nature; nor can I myself grasp all that I am. Therefore the mind is not large enough to contain itself. But where can that uncontained part of it be?'[15] And, he then answered, as have millions of others, that it must be somewhere apart from nature.

Business, too, has a bad reputation because of this, as well as the free marketplace, because if our natural selves are somehow inferior, then servicing it with the vigor with which people in business do must be misguided. People who pursue profit or material wealth, would then be pursuing trivia. They would be mere hedonists. As the title of one of my articles put it, 'Praise Mother Teresa and then Hit the Shopping Malls.' In other words, we live a schizophrenic life. We embrace the value of prosperity, economic success, wealth on the one hand but then we deny it on the other.

Yet, if in our lives we embrace our bodies, minds, emotions, sensations and so on, then we suggest by this that a more integrated view of how to live and how to protect our values is right, not one that tears us into warring pieces.

The private property rights system rests, in part, on such an integrated understanding of human life, not the schizophrenic one. It

---

[15] Augustine, *Confessions*, Lib. X, chap. 17. 8ff

rejects the idea that each human being is divided, a view that much of our literature embraces. It places us squarely on this earth, even though it is by no means hostile to anyone who chooses to look elsewhere for fulfillment, quite the contrary. (Indeed, the right to private property has made religious pursuits extremely fruitful as well as abundant, especially in the United States of America where churches can purchase their own land and welcome parishioners where they will not be disrupted by their foes.

The divided self idea started with Plato, at least with a certain reading of him, where he takes our minds to be divided from our bodies and where the mind is supposed to hold the rest of ourselves in check, to rule it firmly. Countless writers, especially theologians, have ever since stressed this drama and it is reflected in our society's institutions. Victor Hugo made note of this point:

> On the day when Christianity said to man: You are a duality, you are composed of two beings, one perishable, the other immortal, one carnal, the other ethereal, one enchained by appetites, needs, and passions, the other lofted on wings of enthusiasm and reverie, the former bending forever to earth, its mother, the latter soaring always toward heaven, its fatherland — on that day, the drama was created. Is it anything other, in fact, than this contrast on every day, this battle at every moment, between two opposing principles that are ever-present in life and that contend over man from the cradle to the grave?[16]

Even secular thinkers, such as Adam Smith, tended to accept this dichotomization of two sides of the human self when he noted, in his famous remark, that 'It is not from the benevolence of the butcher, the brewer, or the baker, that we expect our dinner, but from their regard to their own interest. We Address ourselves, not to their humanity but of their advantages.'[17] Why juxtapose our humanity with our advantage?

---

[16] Victor Hugo, *La preface de Cromwell*, Maurice A. Souriau, ed. (Geneve: Slatkine Reprints, 1973).

[17] Adam Smith, *The Wealth of Nations* (Indianapolis, IN: Liberty Classics, 1994) page 26-27. But see also Smith's observation, in this very same work, lamenting the very same point at issue here. Smith notes that 'Ancient moral philosophy proposed to investigate wherein consisted the happiness and perfection of a man, considered not only as an individual, but as the member of a family, of a state, and of the great society of mankind. In that philosophy the duties of human life were treated of as subservient to the happiness and perfection of human life. But when moral, as well as natural philosophy, came to be taught only as subservient to theology, the duties of human life were treated of as chiefly subservient to the happiness of a life to come. In the ancient philosophy the perfection of virtue was represented as necessarily productive to the person who

Aristotle and other ancients didn't when they accepted prudence as a *bona fide* moral virtue.

As a result of this popularization of our allegedly divided self, many of us are often apologetic when pursuing a satisfactory, happy life here on earth. And then they find it difficult if not impossible to defend the political regime that most clearly enhances such a life, becoming defensive when others maintain that, well, it is a mundane, materialist life that such a regime supports. Which is probably responsible, more than anything else, for the unrelenting moral disdain exhibited in most cultures toward capitalism, even while as a practical matter the system simply cannot be dispensed with.

Mind you, there are many people with a dualistic bent — e.g., Acton, Cobden, Bright, Bastiat, and Tocqueville — who have favored the liberal political order. That is not at issue here. Argumentatively, however, they are not able to show the morally compelling merits of its capitalist order since they are bound to the view that the pursuits of this world are not so vital to human beings as the pursuits of a supernatural one. Prudence includes concern for economic prosperity as a priority only if the self whose well being is to be looked after is largely the living, actual self of this world. If it is not, if the vital elements of the human self pertain to one's after life, then the moral imperative to seek to prosper in life can easily be undercut with the moral imperative to prepare for the afterlife. This preparation may indeed require foregoing — and has often been urged to supercede pursuing — the prosperity that is possible in this one.

The fact that dualism undermines the case for a free, capitalist, classical liberal order does not mean no dualists have supported one, only that this support has been vulnerable to criticism from within their own frame of reference. That alone is reason why the idea of the divided human self must be seriously rethought.[18] Without serious modification of it, based on the evidence of everyday lives and history, the best socioeconomic system human beings have ever identified will fail to gain moral standing and to flourish.

---

possessed it, of the most perfect happiness in this life. In the modern philosophy it was frequently represented as almost always inconsistent with any degree of happiness in this life, and heaven was to be earned by penance and mortification, not by the liberal, generous, and spirited conduct of a man. By far the most important of all the different branches of philosophy became in this manner by far the most corrupted.'

[18] This is not to say that everywhere the dualist conception of the human self is in vogue, quite the contrary. In most ordinary, practical contexts people think and talk in ways that shows clear awareness of the fact that we are multifaceted, multi-dimensional beings rather than ones consisting only of two irreconcilable elements, mind and body. That latter idea arises more out of theory than practice.

Chapter 4
The Gist of a System of Liberty

Pedigree and Essentials

I began this work with a discussion of the basic elements of libertarianism. I wish to provide now a more developed statement of the position.

Libertarianism emerged from the classical liberal tradition, as a purified or more consistent version of its pedigree. Figures such as John Locke, Adam Smith and John Stuart Mill of the classical period and Ayn Rand, Murray N. Rothbard, Milton Friedman, F.A. Hayek and Robert Nozick from recent times spring to mind as major influences of the position as it is now understood and discussed.

The focus of libertarianism is on the political priority of individual (negative) liberty (i.e., from others' intrusiveness). In the libertarian view the basic rights of every (adult) individual to life, liberty and property are the central normative claims underlying the political, legal, economic and social system most suitable for human community life. Libertarianism stresses the legal fundamentality of the right to private property (where property includes land, inventions, poems, factories, or herds of cattle) since it is by reference to what can be owned that concrete borders — and thus spheres of authority or sovereignty — between individuals can be clearly enough identified. Everyone has the right to seek to obtain and hold, if obtained without rights violations, whatever can be owned.

Although there are several strains of libertarianism, the differences concern mainly the supporting philosophical argument. Some use different terms — for example, eschewing talk of rights, some stress the utility, efficiency, practical value or the progressive prospects of regarding individual liberty as the highest public good. Still, two major views appear to have emerged as prominent: a more or less positivist (or social scientific) line of argument and one that involves mainly normative (or moral) considerations.

Positivist (Economic) Libertarianism

Positivists focus on the common human objective of prosperity or wealth, something preeminently likely in a society wherein private property rights are respected and protected. Prosperity, along these lines, is determined subjectively — that is, by reference to how citizens perceive themselves to be satisfied, enriched, fulfilled, successful, etc.

As in all non-cognitivist approaches to values, this (neo-Hobbesian, *homo economicus*) libertarianism is advanced as value-free. From within this framework, respect for the right to individual liberty — identified as the absence of physical intrusion by others upon the person and property of any individual — would most effectively secure certain progress toward the most widespread satisfaction of preferences.

Normative (Moral) Libertarianism

The normative libertarian takes value judgments to be objective, albeit most often agent-relative (i.e., depending upon many individual, social, and other aspects of the individuals involved). Among these is the central condition — to be secured by everyone within a community — of individual self-determination, personal sovereignty or autonomy. This value, as others, is established by reference to what and who an individual is — in this case by reference to everyone's essential moral self-directedness.

Because the morally successful individual must take the initiative to do the right thing — to act ethically — the condition of liberty (spelled out by the set of basic individual rights) is indispensable for everyone's moral development. Private property is the concrete condition of moral autonomy and political sovereignty — making individual choice possible, for better or worse.

Individualism and Liberty

Individualism — or either psychological or ethical egoism — is crucial in libertarianism, as a step in the argument for it. Some version — not necessarily that referred to (by critics) as atomistic — is closely linked to libertarianism. Personal determination of or responsibility for one's own action — so that the individual person is decisively (though not exclusively) involved in initiating judgment and shaping conduct — is vital. Yet sociability as an essential component of human life — provided it is not coercively imposed — is also compatible with the libertarian vision.

Justice, Equality, etc. via Libertarianism

Whether arising from positivism or a normative approach, the concrete socio-economic result in libertarianism is a polity stressing the supreme significance of the right to individual liberty. Such notions as 'justice', 'equality', 'order', 'welfare', etc. also have a role in the development of the libertarian's basic legal framework or constitution, albeit never superseding the right to individual liberty. Government is thus limited, if it is admitted as proper at all. (Some libertarians, such as Rothbard, are anarchists.)

Libertarian justice consists in a legal system's focus upon the standards of due process that ban involuntary servitude, regardless of how worthy the objective might be (e.g., fighting crime, defending the country, fostering the arts, sciences, health care, education, recreation, etc.). Such objectives needn't lack widespread acceptance or even objective value. Yet, having to reach them without the violation of individual rights (for example, without taxation, universal conscription, state transfer or redistribution of wealth) is the central prerequisite of justice.

Equality, too, is understood by reference to the mutual condition of liberty that every citizen must enjoy — that is, everyone is equal in respect of having the right to life, liberty and property, regardless of whether equality prevails in natural assets, good fortune, health, well-being, sexual appeal, etc. Thus libertarianism tolerates various types of social injustice, such as personal betrayal, economic exploitation, and racial discrimination, so long as no force and fraud is involved. Furthermore, while it is egalitarian at the political and legal levels of community life, there is no insistence here upon the political priority of equality in economic, educational, athletic, or similar opportunities, let alone equality of conditions or results, level playing fields, etc. The main reason is, briefly, that to establish such equalities is seen to require the violation of individual rights. (It is, of course, argued by most libertarians that such equality is a pipe dream — clearly those attempting to establish the equality in question would always fail to be equal to others in the central respect of being authorized to violate individual rights.)

Libertarianism is concerned with political — not social or economic or racial or ethnic — justice and equality. While the latter are not, by at least some libertarian luminaries, incapable of being identified and sought out, they must be pursued without recourse to the violation of individual rights to life, liberty and property. Order, progress, cultural diversity, ethnic, racial and gender harmony are similarly regarded as possibly valid but never primary values for a good political community.

Comparative (Non-Utopian or Idealistic) Assessment

There is no room here to consider the innumerable theoretical objections, let alone aversions, expressed against libertarianism. Put simply, libertarians take most of them to stem from utopian or idealistic thinking.

Indeed, at the level of comparative political thinking the libertarian may be distinguished by a lack of utopianism. (This is especially true of the normative libertarian, who does not see human nature conducive to perfectibility or conceive of any institutional guarantee against immoral conduct — imprudence, dishonesty, stinginess, greed, sloth.)

Accordingly, when it comes to assessing the merits of libertarianism, it is argued that it should be done comparatively: Which polity is most likely or highly probable to do justice to the most rational assessment of the human social good? Utopian or idealistic thinking judges political theories by impossible standards and, thus, encourages misguided public policy and legal measures. Because individuals are fallible and cannot be engineered to be morally good, the utopian aspirations of many competing political, social and economic frameworks need to be set aside. When this is done, so the libertarian holds, the polity of individual liberty comes off as superior to all live options and contenders.

When it comes to the libertarian approach to business ethics what stands out is the principled insistence on the public policy of laissez-faire, not embarking on any type of prior restraint (analogous to the public policy of respecting and protecting the right to freedom of the press or religion). Yet this does not tell the whole story because libertarians see people as not confining their interest to politics alone. As far as libertarianism is concerned, business ethics — albeit not strictly speaking concerned with politics and public policy but with answering the specialized question 'How ought a person embarking on commerce, as an amateur or professional, to conduct himself?' — draws on ethical not political theory. Whatever sound ethical theory human beings ought to live by will have implications for the various roles human beings take on in their lives, including the role they have as commercial or business agents. Libertarianism is not directly concerned with what ethical theory is sound, although in the defense of libertarianism it is usually stressed that commercial and business activities are morally at least unobjectionable if not outright morally proper (as per the exercise of the virtue of prudence in a social context).

Chapter 5

Liberty – Abstract & Concrete

In this chapter I address a potpourri of issues. Some are very general and some are quite specific. The point is to illustrate how a regime that takes the protection of the right to individual liberty as its primary public policy objective would handle them and what view would guide such a regime when dealing with various broad, let's call them constitutional, matters.

Some of the selections were guided by the difficulty of their topic. Some by how controversial they are. Some by the pervasiveness of the problems they raise. But space limitations also prevented my dealing with many other vital topics, such as why it is wrong to ban drug abuse or even traffic in dangerous drugs; how a free society would handle foreign policy; when might war be justified, and how to approach environmental challenges. I deal with some of these matters elsewhere.[1]

Liberty and Abortion

Is abortion to be banned in a fully free society or is the decision as to whether prospective parents will terminate a pregnancy up to them? How might this issue be dealt with in a way that is not specific to some religious faith – in short, in a non-sectarian fashion?

The topic of abortion concerns the killing of what would under normal circumstances become a human infant – indeed, the dispute is about when this occurs. In fact the topic concerns when exactly a human being comes into existence, at conception (whereby all abortions would be homicide), or later (in which case early ones would not be homicide).

---

[1] For example, in my books *The Passion for Liberty* (Rowman & Littlefield, 2003) and *Humanity First, Toward a Sound Environmentalism* (Rowman & Littlefield, 2004).

Just to clarify, 'pro-life' and 'pro-choice' are both misleading labels. They are not at all descriptive. Pro-lifers are not actually supporting life *per se* — for example, they do not oppose killing non-human life, nor killing human beings in self-defense or as punishment. Pro-choicers often want to defend the right to choose in very limited spheres. They oppose government interference in whether a woman continues her pregnancy but not, say, whether she should consume drugs.

Strictly put, libertarians can have no position on abortion as libertarians. This is because the libertarian holds only that whenever a human being comes into existence, killing it in other than self-defense must be prohibited. But some hold that in the first stage of pregnancy pregnant women carry not a mature but only a potential human being, akin to the relationship between a caterpillar and the butterfly it will become, or of a sapling and the tree it will grow into. Some others hold that immediately after conception a fully developed human being, in full possession of all of its human rights, comes into existence. But libertarians have no theory, as libertarians, concerning which of the above views is right. For that one needs to enter into matters that are pre-political.

Here is how the pro-choice position would have it: The claim that a human being exists at conception or prior to the formation of the cerebral cortex seems impossible. Here is why: at conception only a 'pre-embryo' exists. As biologist F. M. Sturtevant points out, this 'consists of the trophoblast, and a few cells comprising the embryoblast.' Indeed, he continues, 'before day 14, when the embryo can first be said to exist, the embryoblast can develop into an embryo proper, a tumor, a hydatidiform mole, a choriocarcinoma (i.e., cancer), twins, or triplets, or, in at least two-thirds of the cases, nothing at all (due to genetic defects).' As Sturtevant puts it, 'until the primitive streak appears at day 14, there is no human individual.' This implies that nothing with a distinctive identity even as a potential human being exists at that stage. Even after the second week an infant human being (unborn child) does not exist. Something that can become one, of course, does.

Does a human life exist at this point? 'Human life' can mean any live element of a living thing, according to which usage any part of the being that will probably turn out to be or has become a human being can be considered living — an appendix, a limb, or any organ one clearly has the option to donate (such as an extra kidney). Even after brain death, for example, the organs that may be transplanted will be live human organs, exhibiting or manifesting human life.

Whether abortion, however, is homicide, let alone murder, depends on whether what is being killed is a human being not just human life. If killing human life alone constituted homicide, than destroying or killing a living human organ, after the death of the human individual whose organ it used to be, would amount to homicide.

Unless it is established conclusively that what is killed via abortion is a human being, the claim that homicide has been perpetrated via abortion is not proven.

Those who embrace the pro-life position hold, in contrast, that since from the moment of conception there is something that can only be classified as having a human identity, one that will last until its death, the being that emerges in however indeterminate way after conception is, in fact, a human being. Some, mainly those who hold certain religious beliefs, argue that at the point when egg and sperm unite, ensoulment occurs — the new entity gains its distinctive humanity, which is to possess a nature with dignity and moral significance.

Those favoring a fully free society need to decide public policy and law based on which of the above arguments, in one or another of their nuanced form, is sound. One thing, however, about the political perspective guiding public policy in a free society seems to favor a secular rather than theological approach to the topic of abortion or, indeed, any other topic. This is that rationales for any public policy in a free society need to be accessible to citizens as such. It would be sectarian and thus biased to rest public policy on elements of a given faith, one that is the province of only those who have been graced to hold it but not to those who have not been so graced.

Yet there are also secular theorists who are pro-life although more who are pro-choice. The pro-life view has several versions and besides what I have sketched earlier there is the consideration that treating the zygote or embryo as if it where a child is logically more prudent than the opposite course. Since we do not know when precisely the cerebral cortex develops in a fetus, the point at which a 'rational animal' would emerge, it is prudent to treat the fetus as fully human from the start of pregnancy.

Pro-choice advocates reply that to be a human being requires a brain that enables something to think, to form ideas, theories, principles, etc., namely, the cerebral cortex. In the fetus this portion of the brain fully develops near the twenty-fourth week of pregnancy. The nearly born, just as babies, however, can and often do think, albeit at the very minuscule level, just embarking on the formation of some ideas — so partial birth abortions, so called, could only be performed in case the mother's life is in serious danger from carrying to full term. But this view implies, if true, that it is unfounded to accuse someone of homicide who has an abortion, or performs one, before the twenty-forth week of pregnancy. To punish such a person for murder or even manslaughter is unjust and laws must prevent such actions. It is comparable to punishing someone for simply not believing something that is false, namely, that the fetus is a human being.

Some hold that a human being does not exist until society can recognize its independent existence, which would be after its birth. They stress that the traditional assignment of birth to emerging from the mother's womb indicates powerfully that it makes little sense to construe any pre-born stage as fully human.

Others argue, with specific appeal to libertarian concerns, that the pro-life position implies extensive law enforcement presence in the lives of couples. This is because if at conception a human being comes into being, then its rights would require protection from the legal authorities, something that would require intrusive monitoring of, for example, the results of all sexual intercourse. Were parties using protection? Did a human being result? Moreover, if miscarriages occur, whether these come about through negligence or even malice aforethought would be of public concern. Gaining the information to make sure no one has been wrongfully killed would involve intrusiveness that libertarians generally abhor.

It needs to be noted that even if one holds that all abortions are not homicide they may not be morally unobjectionable. They must then be legally tolerated, however, because otherwise innocent people would be punished.

The libertarian awaits a resolution of this controversy. Without that, no libertarian stance can be definitive. Banning abortions prior to the twenty-forth week or so of pregnancy may be unjust for libertarians, since it protects no one's right to life, liberty or pursuit of happiness but punishes those who refuse to carry on with a pregnancy, period, which is itself a severe rights violation. But if it is a gray area we face here, perhaps prudence requires that no abortions be allowed, lest we risk killing an innocent child.

Capitalism and Liberty

Capitalism is the political economic system in which the institution of the right to private property, that is, to own anything of value (not, of course, other human beings, who are themselves owners), is fully respected. There is dispute about the label, of course, mostly because its definition is often a precondition of having either a favorable or unfavorable view of the system.

By itself capitalism is an economic arrangement of an organized human community or polity. Often, however, entire societies are called capitalist, mainly to stress their thriving commerce and industry. More rigorously understood, however, capitalism presupposes a type of legal order governed by the rule of law in which the principle of private property rights plays a central role. Such a system of laws is usually grounded on classical liberal ideals in political thinking. These ideals may incorporate positivism, utilitarianism, natural rights theory and/or individualism, as well as notions about the merits of laissez-faire (no government interference in commerce), the 'invisible hand' (as a principle of spontaneous social organization), prudence and industriousness (as significant virtues), the price system as distinct from central planning (for registering supply and demand), etc.

Put a bit differently, 'capitalism' is the term used to mean that feature of a human community whereby citizens are understood to have the basic right to make their own (more or less wise or prudent) decisions concerning what they will do with their labor and property, whether they will engage in trade with one another involving nearly anything they may value. Thus capitalism includes freedom of trade and contract, the free movement of labor and protection of property rights against both criminal and official intrusiveness.

The concept of 'freedom' plays a central role in the understanding of capitalism. There are two prominent ways of understanding the nature of freedom as it pertains to human relationships. The one that fits with capitalism is negative freedom, namely, the condition of everyone in society not being ruled by others with respect to the use and disposal of themselves and what belongs to them. Citizens are free, in this sense, when no other adult person has authority over them that they have not granted of their own volition. In short, in capitalism one enjoys negative freedom, which amounts to being free from others' intrusiveness. The other (positive) meaning of freedom is that citizens have their goals and purposes supported by others or the government so as to prosper. Under this conception of freedom one is free to progress, advance, develop, or flourish only when one is enabled to do so by the efforts of capable others.

In international political discussions the concept 'capitalist' is used very loosely, so that such very diverse types of societies as Italy, New Zealand, the United States of America, Sweden and France are all considered capitalist. Clearly, no country today is completely capitalist. None enjoys a condition of economic laissez-faire in which governments stay out of their citizens' commercial transactions except when conflicting claims over various valued items are advanced and the dispute needs to be resolved in line with due process of law. But many Western-type societies protect a good deal of free trade, even if they also regulate most of it as well. (The extent of such regulation in the United States of America alone, thus the divergence from pure capitalism, is chronicled in *The Governmental Habit*.)[2] Still, just as those countries are called 'democratic' if there is substantial suffrage — even though many citizens may be prevented from voting — so if there exists substantial

---

[2] Jonathan R. T. Hughes, *The Governmental Habit*, 2nd edition [1990].

free trade and private ownership of the major means of production (labor, capital, intellectual creations, etc.), the country is usually designated as capitalist.

The most common reason among political theorists and economists for championing capitalism is this system's support of wealth creation. This is not to say that such theorists do not also credit capitalism with other worthwhile traits, such as encouragement of progress, political liberty, innovation, etc.

Those who defend the system for its utilitarian virtues — its propensity to encourage the production of wealth — are distinct from others who champion the system — or the broader framework within which it exists — because they consider it morally just.

The first group of supporters argue that a free market or capitalist economic system is of great public benefit, even though this depends on private or even social vice, such as greed, ambition, exploitation. As Bernard Mandeville, the author of *The Fable of the Bees*, put it, this system produces 'private vice, public benefit'. Many moral theorists see nothing virtuous in efforts to improve one's own life. They believe, however, that enhancing the overall wealth of a human community is a worthwhile goal.

Those who stress the moral or normative merits of capitalism say the system rewards hard work, ingenuity, industry, entrepreneurship, and personal or individual responsibility, and this is all to the good. This alone makes the system morally preferable to alternatives. Yet, another reason given why capitalism is not only useful but a morally preferable system is that it makes possible the exercise of personal choice, something that would be obliterated in non-capitalist, collectivist systems or economic organization.

The most influential critic of capitalism is the nineteenth century German thinker and social activist Karl Marx. He did not oppose capitalism but argued that it occupies only a specific period of humanity's development. Capitalism, as Marx saw it, is the adolescent period of humanity, as it were. Socialism is the young adulthood, while communism is full maturity. Marx believed that supporters are wrong to assume that the system has universal relevance and validity. Instead, Marx held, the system must be accepted as a temporary fact of the life of humanity — two or perhaps four hundred years long.

Capitalism's defenders have argued, in response, that the system that is based on economic liberty is best suited to human beings because human nature is reasonably stable over time. Human beings, in turn, tend always to be motivated by self-interest or they will always want to be rewarded for their work and will not likely develop into creatures who are loyal primarily to humanity or society, never mind their self interest.

Others have responded to Marx by claiming that not only is his position untenable but actually morally despicable. The vision of human life Marx champions cuts directly against what is best about human beings, namely, their individuality, uniqueness and resulting multifaceted creativity, that is, their often single-minded vision. Capitalism accords more with the idea of human excellence exemplified by the great artists, scientists, industrialists of the world, not the vision exemplified by members of a stagnant commune. Capitalism is feared only by the lethargic or cowardly, who do not prefer the hustle and bustle of nature, including human life.

Capitalism is an economic organization based on some very limited rules or principles. People are at liberty to do everything other than intrude on the sovereignty of other human beings and their authority to make peaceful use of what they own. As such it is a system said to be well suited to human nature, whereby one may embark on various tasks and do well or badly at them but avoid intruding on others. This is best done when one's own sphere of authority — one's private property rights — is clearly identifiable.

Although capitalism is commonly understood in economic terms — 'capital' refers to a vital category of economic resource, namely, what a person or firm has available to use in some enterprise — in fact it is dependent on certain non-economic elements of community life. The basic rights to life, liberty and property, when established, maintained and protected in a legal system, make capitalism possible, although not necessary. If one has the right to one's life, one may exercise this right by offering to spend this life, at least in part, on other people's projects, provided one's terms are met. If one has the right to liberty, one may exercise this by embarking on economic pursuits. And the right to private property is clearly indispensable for purposes of trade — one cannot do that without owning what might be traded. As Abraham Lincoln observed:

> . . . but even these [the US Constitution and the Union] are not the primary cause of our great prosperity. There is something back of these, entwined itself more closely about the human heart. That something, is the principle of 'Liberty for all' — the principle that clears the path to all — gives hope to all — and, by consequence, enterprise, and industry to all.

Although some would reduce all aspects of life to economics, in fact, however, it has several dimensions of which the economic is just one. Capitalism is the economic order of a free society, free in the sense that such a society respects and protects each individual's rights to life, liberty and property.

Government Regulation

In the USA there are two well-known legal principles that are invoked to give government regulation of business legal justification. They are the federal constitutional provision of the interstate commerce clause and the common law provision of the police power of government.

Article I, section 8 of the US Constitution contains the provision that Congress has the power to regulate interstate commerce. The colonies had engaged in various mercantilist economic practices — imposing duties on imported goods, restricting trade, etc. — and this needed to be stemmed.

The police power, in turn, is a legacy of feudalism where the king is responsible for how communities are shaped. This had been imported into American law from England and other European countries.

As to the moral or philosophical support for government regulation, There are essentially four arguments for it: the creature of the state argument advanced by Ralph Nader and his followers; two types of market failure argument invoked by, among others, John Stuart Mill and John Kenneth Galbraith; positive rights to provisions argument advanced by such political philosophers as Alan Gewirth and John Rawls, and the judicial inefficiency argument proposed by the Nobel Laureate economists Kenneth J. Arrow.

Creature of the State: The first argument states that corporate commerce is a creature of government itself — it was brought into existence by acts of the British mercantilist government so as to enhance the wealth of the country. Since government created them, it is authorized and indeed ought to regulated them to accord with the public purpose. Clearly, morally, if one has created something, one is responsible for it and may do with it what is reasonable, responsible.

Market Failures: Although the free market is generally a good provider of goods and services, sometimes it is inefficient. For example, this happens when public services such as the provision of electricity or water is involved. There competition involves duplication and thus inefficiency in the use of resources. So companies should be made into monopolies or taken over by the state. Throughout the world this view has led to the abolition of free markets in some industries and the institution of extensive government regulation of prices, wages, labor relations, etc.

Others have gone further and said government must correct the unwillingness or inability of markets to provide certain services — for example, public libraries, which the market will not furnish. Government regulation, then, is but the legitimate effort of a government to remedy what the market ought to but fails to achieve. We know what these are through the vote. The underlying idea here is utilitarianism — the central obligation of the state is to secure the greatest happiness of the greatest number and when the market fails to achieve this, government must step in with its remedial regulatory policies.

Positive Rights: Some hold that we have basic human rights not only to not be killed, assaulted, or robbed (to life, liberty and property, that is) but also to be provided with various goods and services from other persons around us. This is because the basis of our rights are found in what we need, including from other persons. Without having these needs satisfied, we cannot flourish in society.

The rights to health care, to social security, to public education, to unemployment compensation or to safety and health protection at the work place are examples of positive rights. Government is established among us to secure all these rights and government regulation must be instituted so as to adjust private endeavors so that these provisions will be forthcoming. The argument is really dependent for its force on the theory of positive rights.

Judicial Inefficiency: There are some social problems that privatization cannot solve, namely, some kinds of pollution. When A pollutes the air mass and B suffers as a result of this, neither can A find B so as to secure permission, nor B find A to launch lawsuit. So there is neither a market nor a judicial solution available to the parties. Ergo, government must take over and regulate the sphere of judicially-inefficient human endeavors. (This is not so much an argument for government regulation of business as one for government administration of what some view as unavoidably public spheres.)

What about these arguments, then?

Modern companies are not state created: A fact of history does not establish a moral claim. States used to establish churches and printing presses, yet few defend their authority and responsibility to do so in Western countries, seeing that they should never have done so in the first place. It was learned by bitter experience that the state's sovereignty meant the sovereignty of some people over the lives of other people and so the idea developed that, instead, individuals ought to be recognized as sovereign. And if individuals are sovereign, there is no justification for regulating their lives, be it in commerce, religion, romance, or athletics.

Market Failures: The argument that because some inefficiency may occur in the market, we ought to place the matter into the hands of government ignores individual rights and state inefficiency. When an industry is taken out of the market, competition ceases. Work stoppages or strikes can shut down the entire industry, leading to restrictions on the free movement of laborers. That's too high a price to extract for efficiency and, indeed, far more inefficient over the long haul than are occasional duplication of facilities and resources.

As to the services the market does not always provide, it is once again dubious to suppose that government will supply them in the right proportion, according to a sound set of priorities, effectively, without enormous cost at some other point of the social order. Libraries are now nearly obsolete, except for a few people who could probably be helped much better without building them. Government response to political sentiments expressed in the voting booth is extremely risky since such sentiments are merely voiced, not reconciled with one's budgetary restrictions. Furthermore, the creation of the common pool or valued resources creates a tragedy of the commons, whereby people recklessly overuse resources and create, as is quite evident, huge debts and deficit spending by the state.

The Myth of Positive Rights: We do not have positive rights — because we are not owed servitude from our fellow citizens. Yes, our parents and some next of kin have some responsibility to help us reach maturity. But thereafter we must secure what we need and want by way of voluntary exchange, not government protection of positive rights. These rights are impossible to protect consistently, anyway and, certainly, their protection makes protecting negative rights — our rights to life, liberty and property — impossible. If doctors have the right to liberty but patients the right to be healed, what if the doctor chooses to attend the graduate exercise of his or her daughter but someone in the neighborhood has a right to be healed? Whose right prevails? And on what basis is that going to be decided, now that the system of rights has been corrupted?

Restoring Judicial Efficiency: What of the troublesome case of judicial inefficiency? The problem is not helped at all by government regulation — it merely produces discontent and injustice. Government cannot rationally decide which firm or individual ought to dump harmful wastes on to others' bodies and properties. It cannot establish collective priorities for individuals who are diverse and may flourish in utterly different ways.

Even in public spheres dumping may not be undertaken when no permission can be obtained, unless the result does not increase the prevailing risk of harm to individuals. When manufacturing firms pollute, they utilize other people who did not give their permission for their own purposes. They avoid the full cost of their activities by stealing the resources of others, sometimes even others' lives.

The way to control pollution, then, is to invoke a strict enforcement of personal autonomy and to privatize as much as possible. In areas were this is difficult, a policy similar to what must be done in case of highly communicable diseases needs to be implemented, namely, quarantine.

Generally, government regulation assumes that some people happen to be superior in intellectual and moral gifts than others and that they can be identified and it is wise for them to assume superior powers over the rest of us.

When the government — any branch, any level — regulates, it practices a form of tyranny. It is not the sort we usually dub by that term, unlike ones we know via Soviet (Stalinist) or National (Nazi) socialism. Those were massive, totalitarian tyrannies. The kind where government keeps nagging people in nearly every profession (except those protected by the First Amendment's prohibition of regulation) is more petty, less dramatic, less dire. But it is tyranny, nevertheless.

The reason is actually quite simple: government regulation aims to prevent mishaps by forcing people to act in ways government experts believe are safer, fairer, less difficult to understand than what government believes life should be. It is what we might call a form of preventive justice, by exactly the means that the criminal law prohibits — as noted before, a kind of prior restraint.

The fight against crime does not permit the restraint of people because they might behave harmfully, injuriously, dangerously. Everyone can, even if they will not, choose such behavior. But the law is supposed to punish people only if they have been proven to act harmfully, hurtfully. It is not supposed to second guess how people might behave and then restrain them, not in a free society.

Government regulation of industry, transportation and various other professions amounts to treating people as if the government were our parent who needs to make sure we do not run risks. But the government is not made up of supervisory people, gods, who have the authority to guide what we do in life. Tyrannies do that and they are politically evil. Government regulations are evil, too, in less dramatic ways.

Proponents of government regulation think government must prevent bad things from happening, even if our rights are violated thereby, and the cost is of secondary significance. They see government as upholding principles of justice when it regulates people's activities when they have done nothing harmful but merely could do so.

In a free society it is only once harm is done to others — or when there is a clear and present danger of such harm being done — that government has the authority to act against people's plans, purposes, wishes. The mere possibility of harm is no justification for government action.

Equality and Liberty

The US Declaration of Independence tells us that the founders took it to be self-evident that 'all men are created equal.' Ever since then critics of the idea of the free society have complained that this is nonsense because, in fact, we are quite evidently not all created equal. Indeed, they stress, the truth is we ought to be equal — it is only fair and just. So the role of force in society is not mainly to repel criminal conduct but to make us all equal in all important respects. The kind of equality critics of the American political tradition want is, for starters, impossible. In trying for it one immediately destroys any hope for it, since the enforcers will always be unequal to those at whom their force is targeted.

The only equality worthy of concern, because it is both possible and just, is the kind the Declaration mentions. We are supposed to have been created equal in the respect of possessing the unalienable rights to life, liberty and pursuit of happiness. In other words, we are all rights possessors (except some rare, crucially incapacitated people). That doesn't mean we are equal in our height, fortune, intelligence, looks or talents. Nor, especially, are we all equally well off or even ought to be.

The point of the Declaration's limited egalitarianism is to stress that a distinctive element of human social life is that despite all clear and undeniable differences among human beings, there are some basic principles we ought to respect and protect, namely, our fundamental rights as agents of our choices, ones that in society require this respect and protection. Moreover, when governments are instituted among us, the protection of individual rights is due to each member of society.

Any kind of broader egalitarianism is impossible. That is not, however, how many famous thinkers would have it. Consider the late Isaiah Berlin, who said that 'The assumption is that equality needs no reasons, only inequality does so . . . If I have a cake and there are ten persons among whom I wish to divide it, then if I give exactly one tenth to each, this will not, at any rate automatically, call for justification: whereas if I depart from this principle of equal division I am expected to produce a special reason.'

Yet the case does not prove anything about equality, only about what is expected of one who sets out to divide things among a group, such as what parents do among their children, coaches among team mates, teachers among members of their class and so on. This is because, first of all, a duty exists to care for, train, and teach (respectively) the members of the group in question, not because of the axiomatic value of equality as such. If, in contrast, one gives Christmas gifts differentially, depending, say, on how close one is to the recipient, such giving requires no justification at all, it's taken for granted. Even as one distributes candy on Halloween night, doing it unequally requires no justification — it depends on the age and other apparent attributes of the kids who come to one's door.

Experiences confirm these counter-examples everywhere. Evading them just leads toward undermining that one kind of equality among human beings that is possible and politically right, namely, the equal respect and protection of our rights, one that rests on the prior importance of fulfilling promises or compacts made between the people and their governments!

In any case throughout nature, including human social life, ranking is unavoidable. No matter how much one might wish for it, there will always be better and worse cases of human conduct, institutions, products, and so forth. Not even those who preach full egalitarianism can stick to their 'principles.'

As an example, consider that famous liberal institution, National Public Radio and its various programs. (In Great Britain the BBC would serve as a case in point.) The sheer limitation of time faced in all programming requires selectivity and the elitism NPR practices belies its bleeding heart egalitarianism. The same is true of academic moral philosophy, which is dominated by egalitarian sentiments and ideas. Yet, in practice, academic moral philosophers are very picky about whom they will admit into their ranks. Such academic stars as John Rawls and Peter Singer are, or were, all housed in very highly ranked institutions, despite all their self-proclaimed egalitarianism. And if it were not they, it would be some others. It is impossible to adhere to egalitarianism, period.

We can look elsewhere for even better confirmation of the impossibility of the sort of egalitarianism championed by socialists and welfare statists. Consider how even non-commercial organizations select artists on the basis of some standard — my local non-commercial jazz and blues station constantly features favorites and lists the more renowned artists who take part in various public performances. The symphony in the region must select orchestras and compositions that will be featured. Museums have only so much space available to devote to featured artists. Scholarly journals cannot publish all papers submitted to them. Star systems abound everywhere. So what is available to us is not the kind of impossible egalitarianism socialists and other sentimentalists preach. Rather what we can aspire to is to rank on the basis of valid standards, ones that are difficult to identify but nonetheless our responsibility to discover and apply.

The rest of nature is differentiated mainly by reference to power or fitness for physical survival. Where human beings are different is not in being fit to be cut down to an equal status (on all vital fronts) but in the capacity to make as sure as possible that when they rank, they do it justly, based on merit, desert, competence, achievement and such and that in any case none have their basic rights violated.

Perils of Collectivism

Collectivism includes the various sociopolitical systems that envision human communities as cohesive, even single units, ones with a certain common purpose or goal, akin to how teams or orchestras have such common goals. Harmony, cooperation among all, and progress toward the assigned objective are seen as the great attributes of such collectivist systems — socialism, communism, fascism and the like.

In the case of some animal species collectivism is the norm. Bee hives and ant or termite colonies are such. Their natural and healthy state is absolute solidarity. Other species tend toward collectivism, although it may not be essential for the survival of every member to be united with some group of its kind. Wolves run in packs but can carry on alone, as well, in some circumstances. So the individual wolf is not always a specie-being, what Karl Marx called humans: 'The human essence', he said, 'is the true collectivity of man'.

But collectivism falls prey to the fallacy of composition. It involves lumping individuals into a huge group and ascribing to them capacities, even faculties that only the individual members can have. 'Society says.' 'We decided.' 'America is violent.' Strictly, none of these claims could be true because, to start with, society has no mind and mouth with which to say anything. Nor are we able to decide anything — you may, I may and so may others and together we may reach the same conclusion, including leaving some to do it for us. That is the only sense in which 'we' have decided.

Ordinarily it is well enough appreciated that such expressions amount to linguistic short cuts. 'America is violent' is supposed to mean, usually, that most folks in America are willing to deploy violent means to solve problems. Unfortunately, the care necessary to keep this in mind is not always diligently enough exhibited.

Accordingly, such theorists as Karl Marx explicitly argue that humanity is 'an organic whole.' It is a conscious being in the process of development, with communism its final stage. (Marx talks of the age of ancient Greece as humanity's childhood!) How so, if humanity has no convictions, thoughts, memories, imagination, intentions, purposes or any other attributes that individual human beings do not have? Why is this kind of thinking even plausible?

The reason is that in some contexts human groups nearly become a whole. A close-knit acrobatic team, for example, or orchestra or choir clearly exhibits attributes that come close to incredible single-mindedness. A jamming jazz ensemble not only works as a single musical unit but embarks on the kind of spontaneous innovation that we would usually expect only of individual human beings unencumbered by the baggage of having to please and cooperate with others. But no, sometimes people unite so well, fit so perfectly, and have such a sense of one another's rhythm that it almost looks like individuality has disappeared.

Yet it is precisely individuality that makes such harmonious cooperation possible among members of that acrobatic team, orchestra or choir, and where failures come from, as well — for example, when someone fails to pay close heed to what is needed to keep the unity intact. The complex activities such groups undertake together require the utmost concentration on the part of individual members.

More than even that, when we consider carefully the composition of such groups we note that there is usually a critical mass beyond which they cannot function well. A jazz group can jam but not, say, a swing band — too many people, for one. The same is true with teams and choirs and other human ensembles.

But there is, perhaps, an element of inspiration and hopefulness that is spurred on by witnessing the beauty of harmonized human activities, sometimes to the point of wishing to see it extended globally. When someone like Karl Marx envisions humanity itself acting like an organic whole — as a goal-directed, integrated biological self-propelled organism — he extrapolates from that musical ensemble to all of humanity, convinced that what is possible for the small group could be, indeed ought to be, realized throughout the entire species. So he seriously proposes that we are specie-beings, organisms that belong to the species and form a unity with it all.

Of course, Marx realized that this isn't so at the present and has never been so. But his vision of its vague beauty formed for him a standard of humanity's health and well being, to be achieved in the future and used to judge the present.

The big problem with this vision is that the individuality of every human being can extend to embrace only so many others, after which the fit will be forced and, indeed, must be coerced when its realization is attempted. Human beings are essentially individuals, as well as geared to moderate social entanglements. Voluntary choice reaches out to form only so many social relations. Our emotional make-up does not prepare us to be intimate members of the entire world society, not even of a country. Despite what President Reagan said, America is not a family, nor is Ireland or Iran. Families are sized in just the way that with some attention and vigilance their members can stay close to one another — celebrate birthdays or weddings, mourn the dead, attend to the sick.

If we were the kind of collective beings Marx and other champions of collectivism imagine us to be, we would dry up emotionally. We would lose our capacity to love intimately, to care to be close. We would have to spread our emotional energies way beyond what they are capable of. Just think: circles of friends and families are reasonably sized, so that one is not always torn between sadness about someone's mishap and joy about someone's good fortune. But if we had an intimate relationship with everyone who is part of humanity, nothing could be felt toward others because it would be canceled out by opposite feelings every time.

The kind of community that fits human beings varies a good deal — some are much more gregarious than others. And it must be left to choice to discover how much intimacy is right — how many communities we can honestly join.

The individual's right to choose freely whether to belong to this, that or another group is the best moderator of our social capacities. Sure, we can over- or under-estimate what we are capable of in this as in many other regards. But in the long run it is best to leave it to each of us instead of having some visionaries impose on us an impossible and ultimately destructive social dream.

Liberty and the Democratic State

Democracy (people's rule) is a process by which some decisions are made and in the context of politics it means the kind of system that depends upon the right of participation of the citizenry in public affairs. (The scope of the public realm is, thus, crucial to where democracy may properly be deployed.)

What grounds democracy, as a just mode of political decision-making, is that citizens have the ultimate authority concerning certain matters in the *polis* or their country. And the reason they do have this ultimate authority is that they are, as adults, equal in their status vis-à-vis the stake they have in their political institutions, their laws, public policies, foreign relations, etc.

That they have this equal status hinges on certain extra or pre-political matters, to be discerned by way of reflection upon human nature and proper human relations. For now I will simply note that as I understand political matters, they arise from the moral fact that each individual adult human being has as his or her task in life to choose to live it rationally, to flourish as a rational animal. Since this task for adults can only be achieved if they are not subject to another's will — in which case it is that other's rational choice that would be the ruling principle of one's life — in communities human beings must be sovereign. From this it follows that they must have a say in their own political fate, ergo, democracy.

In any case, democracy is derivative of what human beings are taken to be as they find themselves within a community that aims at justice, a polity. Based on Thomas Hobbes' ideas, democracy is recommended because all of us are equal in being composed of matter-in-motion, lacking any significant, fundamental differentiating attributes. Hobbes held that nothing justifies differentiating some people from others (indeed, if one were to be fully consistent, anything from anything else, at the metaphysical, fundamental level of being.)

A somewhat different reason for democracy arises from the Lockean view. For John Locke we are all equal and independent in the state of nature, i.e., prior to the formation (that is, apart from) civil society. Adult human beings begin as embarking on a human life. In this they are all equal. The life of each individual is to be governed by the laws of nature (which is revealed by one's reason, if one but consults it). So we are all endowed with natural rights, which spell out for each of us a sphere of sovereignty or personal authority or jurisdiction. There are no natural masters or natural slaves (although there may be borderline cases of defective or crucially incapacitated persons). If this is kept in clear focus, one will realize that a human community starts with no one superior or inferior regarding the issue of the authority to make law and to govern. Thus, democracy — a process, morally required by the right to take part in deciding political issues or the right to give consent to be governed. It is not a process that is applicable to everything one might want to influence, however. There is a proper sphere of democracy.

Some propose that democracy is unlimited — only the fact that people will things to be one way or another matters. Some interpreters of Locke have claimed this — e.g., Willmoore Kendall and his followers — as well as some liberals, e.g., Benjamin Barber, and some conservatives, e.g., Robert Bork. They tend to view democracy as a sort of nature community decision-making process to which everyone is naturally obliged to submit.

Yet, for Locke, the justification for government lies in the need for the protection of natural rights, a protection not easily obtained (except by the strong) in the state of nature. So Locke sees the protection of everyone's natural rights as the proper purpose of government. Since establishing, maintaining and protecting government is itself a form of human activity that can be done well or badly, it must be guided by principles. These are our natural rights. The creation, development and operations of government may not encroach upon those rights, lest its proper role in a human community is undermined.

In any case, unless democracy is itself guided by norms — unless the people express and implement their will without violating anyone's rights — it becomes self-defeating. First, there is the problem that such a process is in violation of the rights of innocents who would be made victims of the use of arbitrary force. Second, unlimited democracy can, as noted earlier, undo democracy itself. If democracy, for example, is applied too broadly, it can lead to its abolition — the majority can vote itself out of power. Third, we could democratically vote to exclude some people from the voting process without proper (constitutional?)

limits to the process. If by the democratic process the rights to life, liberty or property could justifiably be abrogated or violated, those taking part in the process no longer can act freely and independently. The majority can threaten their free judgments.

We can extend this analysis now to the realm of contemporary politics in Western democracies. Let's focus on the general situation in the United States of America today. Most people who invoke democracy to justify the myriad of public policy measures that violate individual rights do so only when it supports their agenda. Thus, it is OK to use democracy to rob the rich — it appears to make it valid public policy instead of theft. But if the poor or blacks or women or workers turn out to be outnumbered, then democracy is deemed to have gone too far. The reason is that democracy by itself is never enough for justice. There must always be some specification of those proper goals for which democracy is appropriate. The task of democratic political theory is, in part, to identify those areas of public life that should be subject to democratic decision-making.

What are those areas? And why are they the ones?

Alone or with others, a human being may not do some things to other human beings. No one or group may take over another's life and property. That would amount to murder, assault, kidnapping, battery, rape, or other forms of aggression. The mere fact that the numbers of those who take part in doing the act constitutes a majority makes no difference to the wrongfulness of the act, nor that a democratic procedure has been followed. Without the consent of those whose rights are to be violated, such a process is unjust. It is wrong to steal on one's own as well as with the support of millions. It is wrong to enslave, to place others into servitude when they refuse, etc., no matter whether by oneself, with the minority or with the majority. Nor is it proper for majorities to empower certain people, their political representatives, to carry out such deeds.

Censorship

Strictly speaking, unless the government prohibits or regulates publications or other types of expression of ideas, there is no censorship in a community. However, since most societies contain numerous social organizations that are at least partly the province of government administration, especially primary, secondary and higher educational institutions, indirect censorship is also possible.

For example, if a public high school publishes a student paper and the administration regulates or prohibits what can be published, a kind of censorship occurs. If the high school were a private institution and its administrators spelled out guidelines concerning what may be published and how, this would be more or less sensible internal editing. But since a public high school is administered by the school board, that is an arm of the government, its guidelines, while often sensible enough, cannot escape being censorial. The same goes for such semi-public enterprises as Public Broadcasting Service, National Public Radio, and, especially, the Voice of America, an arm of the US Information Agency. Since there is no fair competition with such organizations their funding from taxes makes their existence immune from the full force of the free market (that is, the choices of consumers), so what they elect to exclude from their array of offerings may be said to have been censored, even if that is far from the intent of those in charge.

Another example of indirect censorship came to light in early 2000. The Clinton White House tried to negotiate a deal with the commercial TV networks concerning the content of TV entertainment. The proposal, kept from the public for some time, was to trade some mandatory public service messages television stations must air (it is one price extracted from them for their license to broadcast) in return for their inserting anti-drug abuse messages into the story lines of television programming directed to kids. The carrot for this had been for the networks to save money by not having to air the unpaid ads.

During a roundtable discussion on PBS-TV several news reporters discussed this topic and while two of them objected not just to the secrecy but to the substance of the deal, two others found fault only with the secrecy while finding the idea of the deal quite palatable. The argument in support went this way: The networks are using public airwaves, the electromagnetic spectrum that had been nationalized on the floor of the US Senate back in 1927 (giving rise to the establishment, at first of the Federal Radio and later the Federal Communications Commission); this empowered the federal government to call some of the shots as far as the use to which the networks will put the signals that travel via the spectrum; so the FCC, and by some perverse extension the White House itself, is authorized to impose terms of usage on network television. QED.

We have here a way government intrudes, via indirect censorship, on the free society via the process of making something public that never should have been made so. Why should government own the airwaves? There is no justification for this. It is socialist governments that characteristically nationalize important resources in the countries that they rule. Socialism is the political philosophy according to which individuals do not even exist but are only dependent parts of the larger whole that is society.

Private property is anathema to socialism. The institution of the right to private property is a concrete, practical implementation of individual rights. It makes the free exercise of religion, of freedom of speech and expression possible for individuals. They can thus act independently of the wishes of others, should they so choose, including the wishes of the government which in such a society has as its proper role the adjudication of disputes about conflicting rights claims. Beyond such adjudication, and the associated legal processes, governments in a free society are supposed to refrain from running the various tasks people may wish to embark upon, including providing entertainment in return for payment or advertising time.

The beginning of the corruption of the proper role of government is the transformation of a system of private property rights into a system of public ownership of valued resources for example, the electromagnetic spectrum that in America had been nationalized in 1927. When this commenced, the rights of individuals begin to be eroded and government begins to set various agendas for society.

In democratic systems this can only be done if a sizeable enough constituency supports these agenda. If the rights of individuals are not firmly respected and protected, the public realm can be increased by way of congressional acts and even presidential edicts. Having nationalized the airwaves, the government can impose various conditions for its use and even undertake underhand deals that would use the broadcasters as propagandists for various goals deemed to be important.

In the USA and many other Western societies, there is a fairly strong tradition of government not exercising its power over the printed media. Radio and television, however, are another matter entirely. In the USA, as noted above, broadcast television and radio are not privately owned. They must obtain a license from the federal government in order to gain permission to operate.

The print media does not face this constraint and is, therefore, more plausibly considered free of all censorship. Thus broadcasting tends to operate with the permission of the state and while such permission is often quite open, programming tends to seem to be uncensored, especially regarding the discussion of ideas. (Even there, however, such measures as the equal access law tend to discourage discussion since high costs are imposed on broadcasters, who must invite opposing views at their own expense.)

Cable television or narrowcasting tends to be free of federal control. But because many of these services are regulated locally, given, for example, special monopoly status and protected from full-blown competition (except from satellite services), they too face a measure of government involvement that can issue in certain kinds of programming restrictions. In some communities, for example, there are restrictions of adult programming to certain times of the day.

In a fully free society government would no more be permitted to exercise power over any kind of expression of ideas, opinions, artistic preferences, and the like than it is permitted to govern religious expression. A complete separation of state and media, akin to the current nearly complete separation of state and religion, would be the status quo.

Some problems do face the theory of total separation, however. One of them is whether any libel and slander laws would exist in such a society. Some argue that because people own their reputation, if others make false charges against them, this constitutes an invasive act, a violation of property rights, in effect. But there are those who find it highly doubtful that anyone owns his or her reputation, given that what other people think of someone is up to those other people and thus cannot be owned. There is also the issue of whether patent and trademark laws constitute some type of grant of monopoly or a valid recognition of ownership based on first creation.

Still, apart from such borderline cases, no government control of the media would be permitted in a fully free society. In other words, since the legal authority would have as its sole task to secure the basic rights of individuals, and since individuals have a basic right to liberty, which includes freely expressing themselves in forums they own or have permission from the owner to make use of, the legal authority would have no basis for embarking on any kind of censorship.

Basically, then, the surest protection against censorship is having the laws focus on the protection of individual rights, especially the right to private property. In socialist systems, in contrast, government owns everything and this gives them total *de jure* control over what is done with the resources available. Without government providing the materials, books, journals, magazines, newspapers, and the various electronic media are unable to function. IF the resources are to be secured, government can set the terms and this basically means nothing gets aired that government considers unsuited for dissemination.

The problem in welfare states, where governments own a sizable portion of the resources needed to live various lives, to carry out various projects, governments can also steer various activities in directions they favor. And the larger the public sector, the more of this 'guidance' is likely, including in the content of the media.

Conscription is Wrong

Conscription is coerced military service, the draft. It requires from young people, mostly men, under penalty of law, the giving up of a portion of one's life, for rudimentary compensation and some reasonably good benefits. In time of military conflict this could amount to requiring someone to sacrifice his life on terms other than his own.

During the presidency of Richard Nixon the draft had been abolished in the USA, with only a faint shadow of it lingering on the law books, the requirement of registration. But instead of championing the completion of the job, namely abolishing registration, some politicians — and Republicans, to boot, such as Senator Strom Thurmond — are enthusiastically and self-righteously favoring bringing back the draft.

The reasoning is not unlike all those in defense of this institution, namely, that 'our nation faces a critical problem of manning our Armed Forces . . .' Of course, no such need could ever justify coercing another person to serve anyone. Sensing that this is going to be a difficult sell, another approach to justifying the draft has been advanced: 'The obligation of mandatory service forces the alignment of self-defense and national defense, of self-interest and national interest.'

No doubt there is much to be said for aligning self-interest and national interest — indeed, any bona fide national interest has also to be in one's self-interest, given how one is a citizen of the nation! But there is a huge flaw in the equivocation between military conscription and the moral responsibility to defend oneself.

No moral obligation may justifiably be forced on a person. One cannot be made to do the right thing, one must do it of one's own free will. The only exception to this is when the right thing involves not violating other people's rights. Then these other people may resist, which is why the criminal law is largely justifiable and why it is also justifiable to force people to refrain from aggression.

In general, a free society is distinguished by virtue of the establishment of a legal system that protects everyone's right to life, liberty and pursuit of happiness. These rights — which the US Declaration of Independence calls 'unalienable', meaning, 'incapable of being lost by anyone' — are nothing if not a major moral obstacle against such measures as military conscription. Such a public policy would be nothing short of enslaving young men and women for portions of their lives. That means their rights to life and liberty would be violated head on.

So in a free society the defense of the country, as any other professional service, must rest on a volunteer military. That is almost a defining attribute of such a community, namely, that its various good deeds must be pursued through consent and not by means of coercion, 'mandatory service.'

Politicians who champion conscription need to come to grips with this fact: one may not achieve good ends by evil means. And it would be evil to defend the freedom of American citizens by means of robbing some of those citizens of their freedom. That, as Sherlock Holmes would put it, is elementary.

The trouble is that recruiting young people for the military in times of relative peace is difficult, especially when government spends its resources on thousands of projects it shouldn't embark upon at all. It requires vigilance on the part of those who believe in military readiness. Given that the vigilance with which a country must be defended should not include making laws to impose involuntary servitude upon US citizens but of the effective advocacy of and ample support for those who would provide defense readiness.

Moreover, as with most professional services, this one, too, can be secured via the free exchange. Government often needs to have things built for it, such as court houses or police stations, and to do this it hires people from the free market and pays them to do the task at hand. Without court houses the legal system would suffer, yet the skilled labor required to build those building may not be conscripted. The talent and work needed are hired to do that important job.

Citizens in a free society must secure services they value without violating the rights of others. In such a society, the most civilized of human communities ever conceived, worthy goals must be achieved by means of argument, not coercion, however impatient one might be about going about things that way. Another person's having basic rights to his or her life, liberty and pursuit of happiness means, in part, that if one wishes to enlist that person's support for some task, one needs to be convincing in one's arguments, meet the terms set by potential service personnel and refrain from bullying people to follow one's lead.

This may appear to be contradicted by such legal instruments as the subpoena. Arguably, however, the only valid use of subpoena is when the pursuit of justice in court cannot continue without a particular person or organization's input. Since everyone in a civil society is committed, by definition, to the pursuit of justice, to withhold oneself from testifying under such circumstances would be to go back on one's own word or oath of citizenship.

However, when a vital service can be obtained from anyone and without even the hint of coercion, that is the alternative that is appropriate for a community of free men and women. No one in particular is needed to defend a country from foreign aggression. Any able person fits the job description.

There are, furthermore, certain practical benefits to banning conscription: the case for going into some military operation must be made more convincingly than otherwise, lest the conflict be pursued without a military. It is little wonder, then, that some politicians do not favor the volunteer approach to securing military service. They do not like it that ordinary citizens would have a significant say about whether a military operation or war ought to be conducted.

Furthermore, if a country is as just as it can be, the probability of making the case for its proper defense to its citizens should be considerable, unless those citizens are in some respect perverse, in which case not being defended against outside aggression is the consequence they must live with.

In a free society patriotism is a matter not of blind habit and simple familiarity but of commitment to principle. That commitment is not some empty slogan, not a case of 'my country right or wrong', but a concrete devotion to act justly and to insist that all elements of society comply with the principle in question. In a free society that means, clearly, that in the very pursuit of justice, justice itself must be deployed. No one's rights may be violated in defense of a community that sees the respect and protection of rights as indeed the paragon of justice.

It is also important to keep in mind that a free society has very little for government to embark upon, military defense of the community being perhaps the most important function. There would be little to consume whatever resource government can secure to fund its various (but by comparison to existing systems very few) activities. Thus, having rid itself of a great many expensive projects, the vital service provided by the military would not be difficult to pay for.

It is interesting that no one ever advocates conscripting police officers, yet, it seems to be analogous to the idea that military personnel ought to be forced to offer their services. Part of this problem may be one of communication, of course: it is a bit more difficult to sell people the idea that their work may be needed in some foreign country than selling them on the idea that local crime conditions must be addressed.

No such obstacles serve, however, to justify anything like coercing young men and women into the military. Those who are convinced that a military operation is needed or that a stand-by military is vital to the safety and security of the citizenry must come up with good, convincing reasons to achieve their goals. No shortcuts in this effort, involving the violation of the basic rights the military is sworn to protect, must be tolerated.

In the context of contemporary understanding of how government function, the points raised against invoking conscription might best be put in terms of the requirement of due process. Just as police officers must not deploy unnecessary force in fighting crime, just as courts must obey principles of justice as they conduct trials, just as prison wardens need to make certain that the inmate's rights are protected, so the more general body politic must not lose sight of the fact that it is securing the basic rights to life, liberty and the pursuit of happiness that government, including the military is all about, a process that must itself do justice to that objective.

Environmentalism the Proper Way

Recently I have been watching a TV series on the Discovery Channel called *The Science of the Impossible*. While doing so I was repeatedly reminded of some of the major complaints of environmentalists and how misguided their proposed remedies tend to be.

It is well know that many who are concerned about wildlife preservation and conservation are not champions of large alterations of the environment, such as the building of huge dams or the rerouting of rivers, all for the sake of making various places inhabitable and exploitable by human beings. Although there are many friends of the Tennessee Valley Authority, most environmentalist are not among them. The same goes for the Hoover dam, the massive irrigation systems achieved from colossal rerouting rivers.

Ordinarily I am a great champion of projects that make human life better — more prosperous, comfortable, enjoyable, and safer. But as with everything else, projects that make all this possible can be over the top, where they are likely to bring more grief than joy, especially in the long run. And one way that is very likely is to have governments deploy their customary tool, coercive force, in reaching the desired goals.

Sadly, however, most members of the environmental movement have a distinct preference for leaving the job of caring for the environment in the hands of big government. Somehow, because they tend to be extremists and often embrace philosophies that out-and-out demean human life, indeed, declare it the scourge to nature — as if people were not part of it — they have no confidence in private-sector solutions. Instead most environmentalists urge the empowerment of the state to help them reach their objectives.

Yet, if history be any guide in these matters, those with fondness for a balanced approach to adjusting the world to suit ourselves should be wary of turning to government for help. As the Discovery series so clearly illustrates in nearly every one of its episodes, the only way that some of these mammoth projects that have carved up the world had a chance for being carried out is by enlisting the power of governments.

Take the Panama Canal. First it was the French government that tried to dig it, through some of the most impenetrable regions of the globe. But it failed. So then America, via private firms at first, tried to tackle the job, but they, too, met with great many obstacles and nearly abandoned the project.

Instead of giving up on it as a good business would when costs exceed investments, however, the federal government under Theodore

Roosevelt, got into the picture big time. It didn't simply farm out the job now, which would have risked failure again in light of the enormous expense. No, it assigned it to the Army Corp of Engineers and put a general in charge.

Roosevelt bragged about this revealingly, saying, basically, 'Now he cannot quit the project unless I order him to.' The workers, many hundreds of whom already perished when the French made their attempts, were now also forced to do their work on the orders of the Commander-in-Chief of the American military.

If this informative series, *The Science of the Impossible*, is to be believed, many other massive projects like this one were carried out throughout the globe. (The narrators are all very enthusiastic supporters for them, by the way!) This was not mainly because scientists and engineers could find the means to do them. The most important reason was that governments could tax (i.e. extort) the funds that would otherwise not have been available — free men and women tend not to invest in extremely risky ventures, nor go to work for employers who lack the funding to pay a decent wage as a result.

Environmentalists beware: the private sector is naturally restrained because projects cannot be embarked upon that are financially futile and highly risky in many other ways. Only governments have the power to conscript unwilling labor and expropriate private property — not just taxes but also land, via eminent domain powers, and to avoid accountability when risky projects fail. Thus it is only governments that can go on routine rampages against the wilds.

A balanced approach to treating the wilds — to taming only parts that are reasonably needed by human beings — is to leave the matter to voluntary methods and keep the state away. It is, after all, the nature of civilized human life that it excludes coercive force among men and women. Only when such force is initiated may force be used to restrain and squash it in return. Otherwise it is best to leave things to free choice. And freely made choices aren't going to be able to embark upon massive alteration of the globe, which is why the environmentalism championed by libertarian, free market theorists is the right approach, not one that continues to have confidence in the coercive force of governments.

Right to Bear Arms

Arms are weapons with which to physically overpower others. There are justified and unjustified cases of overpowering others. Self-defense is clearly a case of the former, aggressing upon another, robbing, murdering, raping, assaulting or kidnapping another would be cases of the latter. Not all guns are but most can be arms.

A principle of the legal system of a free society that is directly derived from the existence, respect for and protection of individual rights is due process. No one's conduct may be banned or regulated without it being very probable that such conduct amounts to rights violation.

Ownership of arms by no means implies their unjustified use. The display of arms, in certain circumstances, could, however, constitute a probable cause for being disarmed. If one aims a bazooka from one's front yard at a neighbor's home, especially one with whom one has had some sort of acrimony brewing, that could qualify. In such a case an injunction against the use, perhaps even ownership, of the weapon in question could be justified.

Barring any such circumstance, ownership of arms is akin to ownership of anything else, a case of the exercise of the right to private property, which in a free society would not be violated.

There are those who advance certain kinds of utilitarian arguments against gun ownership and purchase by citizens without any criminal record or similar valid impediments to such ownership. Some probability does exist that arms will be misused more if their ownership is not prohibited than otherwise. Of course, this is true for implements other than weapons.

In a free society the task of law enforcement would be, in part, to stand guard against the misuse of any weapons or other implements, provided such guardianship does not itself violate individual rights. Furthermore, in the absence of the right to private property as applied to arms, the government and criminals would be the only segment of society that would have free access to them. That also creates a likelihood of the successful illicit use of arms. So the utilitarian case is mixed, even if that were all about which we needed to be concerned. Indeed, the empirical data appears to demonstrate that when ordinary, non-criminal people have their right to bear arms respected and protected, violent crime, which includes shootings, go down in frequency, while the increase of restrictions has been accompanied by a rise of such crimes.

In any case, however, rights trump utility, since rights are derived from our very nature as human beings, while that of utility is extremely unstable, dependent on fluctuating needs and wants. In the US the federal Constitution, accordingly — in the 2nd Amendment of its Bill of Rights — bans government control of private arms. The people are said to have the right to bear arms, not only because, as argued here, they have the right to private property in general but also because it is likely that when government bans weapons for the citizenry, its power over the citizenry grows and is likely to be exercised more freely. Indeed, many measures of the government constitute invasions, violations of individual rights, and in justice citizens ought not to be disarmed when coping with these. Not that armed resistance need be their first recourse in the face of such rights violation. However, whatever recourse they do take, it is useful to have their actions backed with the fact that they could defend themselves against an out of control state.

Some have argued that no absolute right to owning guns can be justified. Indeed, they have held it against libertarians that they lack flexibility in these matters and insist on an artificial absolutism. Yet this is not a very convincing point at all. Those who champion a fully free society are not mindless dogmatists, merely principled. Being principled means, essentially, that the default stance on any issue is a basic principle, in this case that of individual liberty. If, as already noted, it can be shown that a clear and present danger exists from someone's ownership of arms, in a free society legal avenues would exist to meet this eventuality. But the first option on the books would be for no one to prohibit anyone else from owning and using arms unless this involves the violation of another's rights.

A full defense of the right to private property and gun ownership would need to address more fundamental matters, of course. But in the present context those fundamental matters are not at issue. The question is how various public policy matters must be reconciled to the truth of basic libertarian principles. Banning guns does not succeed and, is furthermore, shown to be counterproductive. It seems, in addition, to be a grab for power rather than some safety measure imposed by benign politicians and bureaucrats.

In most societies there are now immense public realms, under the administrative authority of governments. Thus, for example, most primary, secondary and higher education establishments are administered by governments. In the course of such administration various policies appropriate to the management of the school in question may be instituted and these will, in the last analysis, amount to government regulation. A ban on weapons in the schools, then, may seem like a case of government violation of the second amendment, although that is by no means clear cut. Instead, this is the result of government having inserted itself into this essentially non-public activity in society which has gained it a foothold in directing people's lives.

In a fully free system, wherein government would only do its proper activities, namely, secure our rights to life, liberty and the pursuit of happiness (property), no bans on guns by government would exist. However, the innumerable private institutions throughout the community could establish rules of their own, including those that would regulate the use of arms. That kind of system, with its built-in provision for a plurality of solutions to diverse problems — which contrast with the insufferable habit government has to use the 'one size fits all' approach — would be in force in a free society.

References

Bardon, Adrian, 'From Nozick to Welfare Rights', *Critical Review*, Vol. 14, No. 4 (2000), pp. 481–501.
Berlin, Isaiah, 'Equality as an Ideal', *Proceedings of the Aristotelian Society*, Vol. 56 (1955–6).
Chamberlain, John, *The Roots of Capitalism* (Princeton, N.J.: Van Nostrand, 1968).
Cohen, Carl, Communism, *Fascism, and Democracy*, 3rd Edition (New York: McGraw-Hill Companies, 1996).
Cohen, Marshall, Thomas Nagel, and Thomas Scanlon, eds., *The Rights and Wrongs of Abortion* (Princeton, NJ: Princeton University Press, 1974).
F. M. Sturtevant, 'Letter to the editor', *The Wall Street Journal*, November 14, 1994, p. A11.
Fiero, Gloria K., *The Humanist Tradition* (multi-volume) (New York: McGraw Hill, 1994–9)
Foerstel, Herbert N., *Banned in the Media* (Westport, CT: Greenwood Publishing Co., 1998)
Frankel, Charles, *The Democratic Prospect* (New York: Colophon Books, 1962).
Frankfurt, Harry, 'The Moral Irrelevance of Inequality', *Public Affairs Quarterly*, Vol. 14, No. 2 (April 2000), pp. 87–103.
Friedman, Milton, *Capitalism and Freedom* (Chicago: University of Chicago Press, 1962).
Gordon, Doris and John Walker, eds., 'Abortion and Rights', Special issue of the *International Journal of Sociology and Social Policy*, Vol. 19, Nos. 3 and 4 (1999).
Graham, Gordon, *The Case Against the Democratic State* (Exeter, UK: Imprint Academic, 2002).
Hobbes, Thomas, 'Good', chapter 6 of *Leviathan* (New York: Collier Books, 1962).

Honegger, Barbara and Martin Anderson, *Military Draft, Selected Readings on Conscription* (Stanford, CA: Hoover Institution Press, 1982)

Johnson, M. Bruce, and Tibor R. Machan, eds., *Rights and Regulation* (Boston, MA: Ballinger Publishing Co., Inc., 1983).

Kendall, Willmoore, *John Locke and the Doctrine of Majority-Rule* (Chicago: University of Illinois Press, 1965).

Keynes, John Maynard, *The End of Laissez-Faire* (London: L. & Virginia Woolf, 1926).

Kurtz, Paul, *Humanist Manifesto 2000* (Buffalo, NY: Prometheus Books, 2000) (part of a series)

Lecky, William E. H., *Democracy and Liberty* (Indianapolis, IN: Liberty Press, 1981 [based on the original second edition, 1896]).

Locke, John, *Two Treatises of Government* (London: Everyman, 1993).

Machan, Tibor R., *Capitalism and Individualism* (New York: St. Martin's Press, 1990).

Machan, Tibor R., *Private Rights and Public Illusions* (New Brunswick, NJ: Transaction Books, 1995).

Machan, Tibor R., *Classical Individualism* (London: Routledge, 1998).

Machan, Tibor R., *Initiative – Human Agency and Society* (Stanford, CA: Hoover Institution Press, 2000).

Machan, Tibor R.,*The Passion for Liberty* (Rowman & Littlefield, 2003).

Machan, Tibor R., *Humanity First, Toward a Sound Environmentalism* (Rowman & Littlefield, 2004).

Malcolm, Joyce Lee, *To Keep & Bear Arms* (Cambridge, MA: Harvard University Press, 1996)

Marx, Karl, 'On the Jewish Question', in *Karl Marx, Selected Writings*, ed., David McLellan (London: Oxford University Press, 1970).

Marx, Karl, *Das Kapital* (New York: International Publishers, 1967).

Mitnick, Barry M., *The Political Economy of Regulation* (New York: Columbia University Press, 1980)

Nagel, Thomas, *Equality and Partiality* (New York: Oxford University Press, 1991).

Norton, David L., *Personal Destinies: A Philosophy of Ethical Individualism* (Princeton, NJ: Princeton University Press, 1976).

Pols, Edward, *Acts of our Being: A reflection on agency and responsibility* (Amherst: University of Massachusetts Press, 1982).

Rand, Ayn, *Atlas Shrugged* (New York: Random House, 1957)

Rand, Ayn, *Capitalism: The Unknown Ideal* (New York: New American Library, 1966).

Sen, Amartya, *Inequality Reexamined* (Cambridge MA: Harvard University Press, 1992).

Smith, Adam, *The Wealth of Nations* (Oxford: Clarendon Press, 1976).

Stay, Byron L., ed., *Censorship: Opposing Viewpoints* (??: Greenhaven Press, 1992)

Thomson, Judith Jarvis , 'A Defense of Abortion.' *Philosophy and Public Affairs* 1 (1971): 47-66.
Tibor R. Machan, 'Fetal Rights: The Implication of a Supposed Ought', *Liberty*, July 1989, pp. 51-52.
von Hayek, F. A., ed., *Capitalism and the Historians* (Chicago: University of Chicago Press, 1954).
von Mises, Ludwig, *Socialism* (London: Jonathan Cape, Ltd., 1936)
von Mises, Ludwig, *The Anti-Capitalist Mentality* (Princeton, N.J.: Van Nostrand, 1956).

SOCIETAS: essays in political and cultural criticism

- Vol.1 Gordon Graham, *Universities: The Recovery of an Idea*
- Vol.2 Anthony Freeman, *God in Us: A Case for Christian Humanism*
- Vol.3 Gordon Graham, *The Case Against the Democratic State*
- Vol.4 Graham Allen MP, *The Last Prime Minister*
- Vol.5 Tibor R. Machan, *The Liberty Option*
- Vol.6 Ivo Mosley, *Democracy, Fascism and the New World Order*
- Vol.7 Charles Banner/Alexander Deane, *Off with their Wigs!*
- Vol.8 Bruce Charlton/Peter Andras, *The Modernization Imperative*
- Vol.9 William Irwin Thompson, *Self and Society* (March 2004)
- Vol.10 Keith Sutherland, *The Party's Over* (May 2004)
- Vol.11 Rob Weatherill, *Our Last Great Illusion* (July 2004)
- Vol.12 Mark Garnett, *The Snake that Swallowed its Tail* (Sept. 2004)
- Vol.13 Raymond Tallis, *Why the Mind is Not a Computer* (Nov. 2004)
- Vol.14 Colin Talbot, *The Paradoxical Primate* (Jan. 2005)
- Vol.15 J.H. Grainger, *Tony Blair and the Ideal Type* (March 2005)
- Vol.16 Alexander Deane, *The Great Abdication* (May 2005)
- Vol.17 Neil MacCormick, *Who's Afraid of a European Constitution* (July)
- Vol.18 Larry Arnhart, *Darwinian Conservatism* (September 2005)
- Vol.19 Paul Robinson, *Doing Less With Less: Britain more secure* (Nov. 2005)
- Vol.20 Alan and Marten Shipman, *Knowledge Monopolies* (January 2006)
- Vol.21 Kieron O'Hara, *The Referendum Roundabout* (March 2006)
- Vol.22 Henry Haslam, *The Moral Mind* (May 2006)
- Vol.23 Richard Ryder, *Putting Morality Back Into Politics* (July 2006)
- Vol.24 Alice Andrews, *An Evolutionary Mind* (September 2006)
- Vol.25 John Papworth, *Village Democracy* (November 2006)

Public debate has been impoverished by two competing trends. On the one hand the trivialization of the media means that in-depth commentary has given way to the ten second soundbite. On the other hand the explosion of knowledge has increased specialization, and academic discourse is no longer comprehensible. As a result writing on politics and culture is either superficial or baffling.

This was not always so — especially for political debate. The high point of the English political pamphlet was the seventeenth century, when a number of small printer-publishers responded to the political ferment of the age with an outpouring of widely-accessible pamphlets and tracts. But in recent years the tradition of the political pamphlet has declined—with most publishers rejecting anything under 100,000 words. The result is that many a good idea ends up drowning in a sea of verbosity. However the introduction of the digital press makes it possible to re-create a more exciting age of publishing. *Societas* authors are all experts in their own field, but the essays are for a general audience. Each book can be read in an evening. The books are available retail at the price of £8.95/$17.90 each, or on bi-monthly subscription for only £5/$10. Details/updated schedule at **imprint-academic.com/societas**

EDITORIAL ADVISORY BOARD

Prof. Jeremy Black (Exeter); Prof. Robert Grant (Glasgow); Prof. John Gray (LSE); Prof. Robert Hazell (UCL); Prof. Anthony O'Hear (Bradford); Prof. Nicholas Humphrey (LSE); Dr. Efraim Podoksik (Hebrew Univ., Jerusalem).

IMPRINT ACADEMIC, PO Box 200, Exeter, EX5 5YX, UK
Tel: (0)1392 841600   Fax: (0)1392 841478   sandra@imprint.co.uk

The Case Against the Democratic State
Gordon Graham

We are now so used to the state's pre-eminence in all things that few think to question it. This essay contends that the gross imbalance of power in the modern state is in need of justification, and that democracy simply masks this need with an illusion of popular sovereignty. Although the arguments are accessible to all, it is written within the European philosophical tradition. The author is Professor of Moral Philosophy at the Uniiversity of Aberdeen. 96 p., £8.95/$17.90

The Snake that Swallowed its Tail
Mark Garnett

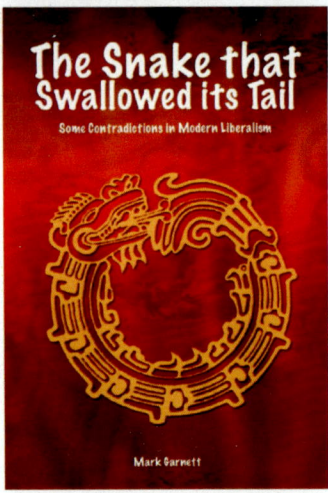

Liberal values are the hallmark of a civilised society. Yet they depend on an optimistic view of the human condition, Stripped of this essential ingredient, liberalism has become a hollowed-out abstraction. Tracing its effects through the media, politics and the public services, the author argues that hollowed-out liberalism has helped to produce our present discontent. Unless we stop boasting about our values and try to recover their essence, liberal society will be crushed in the coils of its own contradictions.   96 pp., £8.95/$17.90

The Party's Over
Keith Sutherland

The book argues that the tyranny of the modern political party should be replaced by a mixed constitution in which advocacy is entrusted to an aristocracy of merit, and democratic representation is achieved via a jury-style lottery. 200 pp., £8.95/$17.90

- *'An extremely valuable contribution–a subversive and necessary read.'* **Graham Allen MP**, *Tribune*
- *'His analysis of what is wrong is superb . . . No one can read this book without realising that something radical, even revolutionary must be done.'* **Sir Richard Body**, *Salisbury Review*
- *'A political essay in the best tradition: shrewd, erudite, polemical, partisan, mischievous and highly topical.'* **Contemporary Political Theory**

Darwinian Conservatism
Larry Arnhart

Darwinian biology sustains conservative social thought by showing how the human capacity for spontaneous order arises from social instincts and a moral sense shaped by natural selection in human evolution.

Larry Arnhart is a professor of political science at Northern Illinois University. He is the author of *Aristotle on Political Reasoning*, *Political Questions: Political Philosophy from Plato to Rawls*, and *Darwinian Natural Right: The Biological Ethics of Human Nature*.

96 pp., £8.95/$17.90

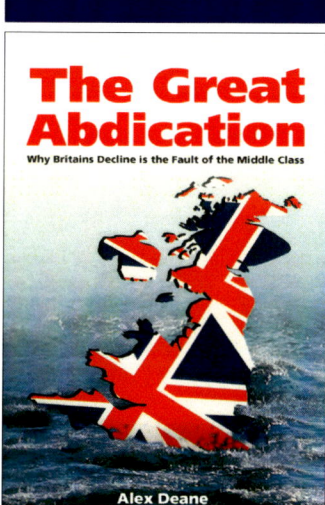

The Great Abdication
Alexander Deane

Our middle class has abstained from its responsibility to uphold societal values, and the enormously damaging collapse of our society's norms and standards is largely a result of that abdication. The institutions of political and social governance provide a husk of functionality and mask these problems for those that do not wish to see, or do not care. To restore Britain to something resembling a substantively functioning country, the middle classes must reinstate themselves as arbiters of morality, be unafraid to judge their fellow men, and follow through with the condemnation that necessarily follows when individuals sin against common values.

96 pp., £8.95/$17.90

The Moral Mind
Henry Haslam

Haslam shows how important the moral sense is to the human personality and exposes the weakness in much current thinking that suggests otherwise. His goal is to help the reader to a mature and confident understanding of the moral mind, which constitutes an essential part of what it is to be human. The author writes from from a Judaeo-Christian background and addresses both believers and non-believers.

96 pp., £8.95/$17.90

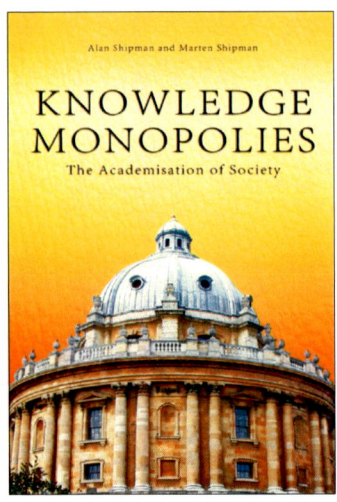

Knowledge Monopolies
Alan Shipman and Marten Shipman

Historians and sociologists chart the *consequences* of the expansion of knowledge; philosophers of science examine the *causes*. This book bridges the gap. The focus is on the paradox whereby, as the general public becomes better educated to live and work with knowledge, the 'academy' increases its intellectual distance, so that the nature of reality becomes more rather than less obscure.

96 pp., £8.95/$17.90

The Referendum Roundabout
Kieron O'Hara

A lively and sharp critique of the role of the referendum in modern British politics. The 1975 vote on Europe is the lens to focus the subject, and the upcoming referendum on the European constitution is also clearly in the author's sights.

Kieron O'Hara is author of *Trust: From Socrates to Spin* (2004) and *After Blair: Conservatism Beyond Thatcher* (2005) and *Plato and the Internet* (2002).

96 pp., £8.95/$17.90

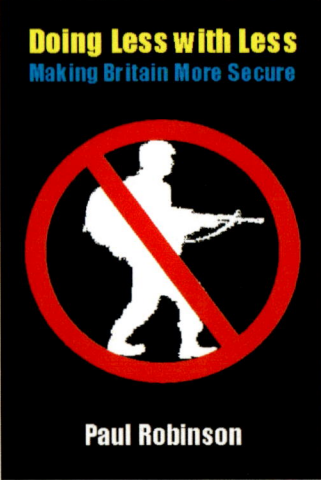

Doing Less With Less
Making Britain More Secure
Paul Robinson

Don't believe neoconservative rhetoric on the 'war on terror': the twenty first century will be much safer. Armed forces designed for the cold war (and only maintained by vested interests within the defence bureaucracy) encourage global interference through pre-emption and other forms of military interventionism. We would be safer with less.

Paul Robinson has served as an army officer and is currently assistant director of the Centre for Security Studies at the University of Hull. His books include *The Just War in Comparative Perspective* (2003).

96 pp., £8.95/$17.90